BATMAN
the black mirror
Jock '10

SCOTT SNYDER
Writer

JOCK
FRANCESCO FRANCAVILLA
Artists

DAVID BARON
FRANCESCO FRANCAVILLA
Colorists

JARED K. FLETCHER
SAL CIPRIANO
Letterers

JOCK
Collection Cover

BATMAN CREATED BY BOB KANE

THE BLACK MIRROR

BATMAN: THE BLACK MIRROR

DC Comics, 1700 Broadway,
New York, NY 10019
A Warner Bros. Entertainment Company
Printed by RR Donnelley, Salem, VA, USA. 1/25/13. First Printing.
ISBN:978-1-4012-3207-8

Certified Chain of Custody
At Least 20% Certified Forest Content
www.sfiprogram.org
SFI-01042
APPLIES TO TEXT STOCK ONLY

Library of Congress Cataloging-in-Publication Data

Snyder, Scott.
Batman : the black mirror / Scott Snyder, Jock, Francesco Francavilla.
p. cm.
"Originally published in single magazine form in Detective Comics 871-881."
ISBN 978-1-4012-3207-8
1. Graphic novels. I. Jock, 1972- II. Francavilla, Francesco. III. Title. IV. Title: Black mirror.
PN6728.B36S67 2012
741.5'973—dc23

2012023707

STORY SO FAR

In the aftermath of the universe-shattering events known as the Final Crisis, Gotham City's Dark Knight was presumed dead.

With the mantle of the Bat unclaimed and the city unprotected, original Robin Dick Grayson took up the cape and cowl as Gotham's new Batman, joined by Bruce Wayne's son Damian as Robin. The two formed a new and decidedly different dynamic duo, while former sidekick Tim Drake assumed the identity Red Robin.

But when a very much alive Bruce Wayne reappears, he does not immediately return to his old role as Gotham's Caped Crusader. Instead, the original Dark Knight sets out on a larger mission: Batman, Incorporated. Recruiting allies around the world, Bruce forms a franchise of Batmen to protect the entire globe.

And the burden of protecting Gotham City is once again left on the shoulders of protégé Dick Grayson...

the black mirror
Jock 10

When I was a boy, my parents kept a **big map** of the country tacked to the wall of our dressing room.

The map had pins stuck in all the places our troupe was going to stop that season.

Different towns and cities were marked with different color pins.
Blue pins meant small towns...which meant small shows, less dangerous tricks.
Red pins meant big cities. So, big shows and more dangerous tricks.
All the stops were marked red or blue...
POOL
...except for one--**Gotham City,** which was marked by a **black pin.**

According to my father, the black pin meant **no holds barred.** Pull out all the stops. Bring down the house.
It meant put on the biggest, riskiest show of the season. No catch wires. No safety nets. Everyone pushing themselves to the **limit.**
I remember one time I asked my father **why.** What made Gotham so **special?**
And my father, he looked down at me, and he said...
"...some places just have a **hunger** about them, son.
"And you either feed them what they want..."

"...or you stay far, far away."
DETECTIVE COMICS presents
BATMAN
in
THE BLACK MIRROR
part ONE of THREE
SCOTT SNYDER writer
JOCK artist & cover
DAVID BARON colors
JARED K. FLETCHER letters

I've felt it many times myself, that hunger...
...the way Gotham will start pulling at you when it wants something, when it wants more...
...it's been feeling like that a lot lately. Wild and strange, and most of all--hungry.
TROUBLE SLEEPING AGAIN, MASTER RICHARD?
I SUPPOSE THAT DEPENDS ON WHETHER WE'RE SEEING THE SAME THING THROUGH THIS WINDOW, ALFRED.
IF YOU MEAN THE VULTURES, SIR, I IMAGINE WE ARE.
SO I'M NOT DREAMING, WHICH WOULD MAKE THE ANSWER YES, I AM STILL HAVING TROUBLE SLEEPING...
NO IDEA WHERE THEY CAME FROM, I TAKE IT?
I'M AFRAID NOT.
SHALL I HAVE THE BED CHANGED AGAIN, SIR?

NO, DON'T BOTHER. AT THE END OF THE DAY, I GUESS I'M JUST NOT THE PENTHOUSE TYPE.
YOU KNOW I ACTUALLY SLEEP WORSE IN THIS PLACE NOW THAT BRUCE IS BACK?
IF I MAY, MASTER RICHARD...THIS IS YOUR RESIDENCE NOW. IT MIGHT HELP TO MAKE IT MORE... YOUR OWN?
I DO HAVE THAT GREAT PHOTO OF ME AND THE ANTI-MONITOR I COULD FRAME. AND IF I HUNG MY OLD PIXIE BOOTS ON THE MANTEL...
JOKE IF YOU MUST, SIR, BUT IT'S BEEN WELL OVER A YEAR SINCE YOU'VE MOVED IN, YET THERE'S BARELY A TRACE OF YOU ANYWHERE.
COME ON, ALFIE, YOU KNOW ALL MY JUNK COULDN'T FILL ONE WALL IN THIS PLACE. NOW TELL ME YOU DIDN'T COME UP HERE JUST TO TALK INTERIOR DESIGN.
FORTUNATELY NOT, SIR... COMMISSIONER GORDON RANG THIS MORNING. HE INQUIRED ABOUT USING THE CRIME LAB.
HUH...SO HE FINALLY CAME AROUND. I TAKE IT TIM'S GIVING HIM THE TOUR?
I'M AFRAID HE'S SITTING IN ON A CONFERENCE. AND WITH MASTER BRUCE OUT OF TOWN, MASTER TIMOTHY THOUGHT IT BEST THAT YOU ACCOMPANY THE COMMISSIONER.
"ALL RIGHT, I'M GOING. JUST DO ME A FAVOR AND CALL SOMEONE ABOUT THOSE THINGS, WILL YOU?"
"OF COURSE, SIR. I DON'T IMAGINE THAT THEIR PRESENCE INSPIRES MUCH CONFIDENCE."

The lab was Tim's idea, of course.
He figured that with Wayne Industries offering funding to Batman, it'd be a slap in the face to the G.C.P.D. not to extend help to the department, too.
So after Bruce's return, Wayne Industries opened a new, state-of-the-art forensic lab, and made the facility available to the G.C.P.D., free of charge.
GOOD TO SEE YOU AGAIN, COMMISSIONER. SO WHAT DO YOU THINK?
WELL, IT'S CERTAINLY SHINY, MR. GRAYSON.
CALL ME DICK, PLEASE. YOU DROVE ME TO MY HIGH SCHOOL PROM.
ACTUALLY I DROVE MY DAUGHTER TO HER HIGH SCHOOL PROM. YOU JUST HAPPENED TO BE IN THE CAR.
FAIR ENOUGH. HOW CAN I HELP, COMMISSIONER?
I TAKE IT YOU HEARD ABOUT THE INCIDENT AT GOTHAM PREP YESTERDAY?
THE POOL ATTACK? JUST WHAT WAS IN THE PAPERS.

That was nearly seven weeks ago. And the G.C.P.D. still hasn't sent a single evidence bag our way...until today.
So, my question is-- why now?
THE TWELVE-YEAR-OLD BOY WHO ATTACKED THE OTHERS-- DANA REDFORD. WE FOUND THIS IN HIS LOCKER. IT'S A HORMONAL MUTAGEN. CAUSES WHAT'S KNOWN AS RAPID, ATAVISTIC REGRESSION.
A KIND OF REVERSE EVOLUTION. WE FIRST ENCOUNTERED THE STUFF A FEW YEARS AGO, WHEN IT WAS GIVEN TO--
KILLER CROC... I REMEMBER READING ABOUT IT IN THE BLUDHAVEN P.D. FILES. TOOK A GUY WITH A SKIN CONDITION AND BAD TEETH, TURNED HIM INTO A GENUINE MONSTER.

EXACTLY. HERE... THIS IS THE ORIGINAL MUTAGEN USED ON CROC. I THOUGHT YOU MIGHT BE ABLE TO RUN A QUICK COMPARISON.
SEE IF THE STUFF DANA REDFORD INGESTED IS FROM THE SAME BATCH.
OF COURSE. IT'S ABOUT TIME SOMEONE PUT THIS CIRCUS TO GOOD USE, ANYHOW.
LISTEN, DICK. ABOUT THAT--YOU WAYNES HAVE MADE A GENEROUS GESTURE, OPENING THIS PLACE UP.
BUT I WOULDN'T HOLD YOUR BREATH FOR MORE BUSINESS, IF I WERE YOU. HUMBLE THE G.C.P.D. IS NOT.
GOOD TO KNOW.
ALL RIGHT, HERE WE GO. LIGHTS, CAMERA... MUTAGEN.
MATCH
SEEMS BOTH SAMPLES ARE FROM THE SAME BATCH. SO I GUESS THE QUESTION NOW IS: HOW DID THIS KID, REDFORD, GET HIS HANDS ON HIGHLY DANGEROUS--
POLICE EVIDENCE?
I WAS GOING TO SAY "RESTRICTED MATERIAL," COMMISSIONER.
WELL, I APPRECIATE THE GOOD MANNERS. BUT AS POLICE YOURSELF...

"...I IMAGINE NOW YOU UNDERSTAND WHY I CAME TODAY. SENDING STOLEN POLICE EVIDENCE TO CENTRAL PROCESSING COULD SET OFF SOME BELLS."
"I CAN PROMISE YOU, COMMISSIONER, WE'RE GOOD AT DISCRETION OVER HERE.
"SO WHAT DID THE KID HAVE TO SAY ABOUT WHERE HE GOT THE STUFF?"
"HE CAN'T SAY ANYTHING. AFTER PUTTING THREE STUDENTS IN THE I.C.U., HE COLLAPSED.
"THE SERUM WAS TOO MUCH FOR HIS SYSTEM--HE'S IN A MEDICALLY INDUCED COMA WHILE THE STAFF AT GOTHAM PRESBYTERIAN TRY TO EXTRACT THE STUFF."
"AND THE PARENTS?"
"JUST A MOM. GALE REDFORD. PROFESSIONAL SOCIALITE. OFF GALAVANTING AROUND SOMEWHERE IN ICELAND WHILE HER KID'S HANGING BY A THREAD.
"ONLY PERSON WHO SHOWED UP TO SEE THE BOY IN THE I.C.U. SO FAR IS THE DAMN BUTLER. NAME OF 'CARSON READ.'
"ACTUALLY SEEMED PRETTY BROKEN UP ABOUT THE WHOLE THING.
"GO FIGURE. KID'S PRACTICALLY RAISED BY THE BUTLER...AND PEOPLE ACT SURPRISED WHEN HE GOES OFF THE DEEP END.
"...NO OFFENSE, OF COURSE."
"NONE TAKEN, COMMISSIONER."

WE SHOULD TALK, MR. READ.

THE MUTAGEN DANA TOOK WAS HIGHLY GUARDED POLICE EVIDENCE.
THERE'S NO WAY HE COULD HAVE GOTTEN IT WITH-OUT *HELP*.
I'VE TOLD YOU EVERYTHING I COULD, SIR. I HAVE...
YOU'RE THE EYES AND EARS OF THIS HOUSEHOLD.
THINK *HARDER*.
IF I KNEW ANYTHING ELSE, DON'T YOU THINK I'D SAY SO?
I PRACTICALLY RAISED THAT BOY MYSELF. HAVE YOU ANY IDEA WHAT IT'S LIKE FOR ME, SEEING HIM HURT AND HELPLESS, LYING THERE?
YES, I THINK I DO.

THE BOY'S MOTHER... IS THERE ANYONE SHE'S COME INTO CONTACT WITH RECENTLY WHO COULD HAVE SOME *CONNECTION* TO THIS?
I... I DON'T KNOW. SHE'S BEEN VERY PRIVATE THE LAST FEW MONTHS. TRAVELING MORE...
I SUPPOSE THE ONE--
CLICK
BOOOM
BAT IN MY HOUSE! BAT!

BAT! BAT!
SHHUNK
BAT IN MY HOUSE! IN MY HOUSE!
MRS. REDFORD! WAIT!

10/6
10/6

IT'S AN OLD DESIGN. JERVIS TETCH'S NEW GENERATION OF TAGS USES FLUNITRAZEPAM AND NILIUM...
...DESIGNER HYPNOTICS THAT GIVE A SKILLED MANIPULATOR A HIGHLY NUANCED DEGREE OF CONTROL OVER HIS VICTIMS.
THE TAG SEWN INTO GALE REDFORD'S NECK IS TREATED WITH A SIMPLE BENZODIAZEPINE DERIVATIVE, WHICH ONLY ALLOWS FOR A CRUDE KIND OF MANIPULATION.
MORE OF A BRAINWASH THAN A REPROGRAMMING.
WHICH WOULD EXPLAIN WHY WHOEVER PUT THE DAMN THING IN MRS. REDFORD'S NECK HAS BEEN KEEPING HER OUT OF THE PUBLIC EYE THE LAST COUPLE OF MONTHS...
THE TAG WAS ADMITTED INTO POLICE EVIDENCE AROUND THE SAME TIME AS THE CROC MUTAGEN. WHEN I CHECKED, I FOUND--
THAT THE SAME OFFICER, CULLEN BUCK, WAS ON EVIDENCE AND PROPERTY FOR BOTH ACQUISITIONS...
SEEMS WE WERE DIGGING IN THE SAME DIRTY SANDBOX, DETECTIVE.

PROBABLY IS. HE TOOK UP WITH AN EX-COP A FEW MONTHS AGO. BECCA MULCAHEY. SHE USED TO RUN WITH JIM CORRIGAN...
SIGH
ANOTHER OF GOTHAM'S FINEST.
WORD IS, THE TWO LOVEBIRDS BOUGHT A TOWNHOUSE OVER ON PARK AND 23rd. WARMS YOUR HEART, DOESN'T IT?
I ALREADY PAID A VISIT TO BUCK'S GOTHAM APARTMENT. THE PLACE LOOKED ABANDONED.
10/6

YOU WANT MY GUESS, THE HAPPY COUPLE IS SELLING SOME OF THE DEPARTMENT'S MORE VALUABLE EVIDENCE ON THE BLACK MARKET.
CLICK
MAYBE. BUT THE MAD HATTER TAG WAS SURGICALLY GRAFTED INTO GALE REDFORD'S NECK. THE WHOLE THING FEELS BIGGER AND SMARTER THAN A THUG LIKE BUCK.
WISH I COULD SAY I DON'T AGREE...
SOMETHING WRONG, COMMISSIONER?
NO... I SUPPOSE I'M JUST NOT USED TO IT YET.
USED TO *WHAT?*
TO YOU STILL BEING THERE WHEN I LOOK UP.

Cullen Buck's new home is
pressive for someone supposedly
iving on a Gotham cop's salary.
He and Mulcahey have filled it with nice things...
...especially **weapons.**
I've spotted everything from Glocks to MK-51's and back again.
Equipment, too. All kinds. I even spied a couple pairs of night vision goggles in the closet.
Generation three, too. Gallium arsenide photo cathode. 51-64 resolution. The kind Special Forces uses...
In other words... compared to mine...?
Kid stuff.

THIS IS MY HOME, YOU CIRCUS FREAK! LET ME GO!
SEE, ME LETTING YOU GO IS EXACTLY WHAT YOU WANT TO AVOID, OFFICER BUCK.
NOW. IT SEEMS CERTAIN THINGS HAVE A HABIT OF DISAPPEARING FROM THE EVIDENCE ROOM UNDER YOUR WATCH.
DANGEROUS THINGS...BELONGING TO SOME OF GOTHAM'S MORE NOTORIOUS RESIDENTS. WHICH MEANS--
HANDS BEHIND YOUR HEAD! NOW!
I SAID NOW!
WELL, WELL. NOT SO TOUGH NOW, ARE YOU, PUNK? WE GOT YOU, WE GOT--
PFFT

BAT-TASER.
YOU WERE SAYING?
YOU DON'T UNDERSTAND. HE KNOWS EVERY-ONE...H-HE'LL *KILL* ME.
HE'S PROBABLY WATCHING US *RIGHT NOW.*
WHO?

LOOK, I DON'T KNOW... I DON'T KNOW HIS NAME. HE'S JUST "THE DEALER." RUNS AN OPERATION CALLED MIRROR HOUSE
>COUGH<
HE COLLECTS THE VILLAIN STUFF, THEN SELLS IT TO THE HIGHEST BIDDER AT THESE UNDERGROUND AUCTIONS. REAL WEALTHY PEOPLE...
>COUGH<
>COUGH<
BUCK?
BUCK, STAY CALM...
GGGGAAKK
BUCK!

My father was right. Gotham is a hungry, wild and deadly place. When it wants something, you hand it over, or you **beware.**
But the same is true of **Batman...**
...and this is the third person I've watched die in front of me this week.
All because of this man, this **"Dealer."**
So I hope he **is** watching, just like Buck said. Because he should know--I'm coming for him.
And when I find him, I'm going to bring the whole house down on top of him.

BATMAN in
DETECTIVE
COMICS
THE BLACK MIRROR
part TWO of THREE
SCOTT SNYDER writer
JOCK artist & cover
DAVID BARON colors
JARED K. FLETCHER letters
The man in the car is William Rhodes.
CFO of Rhodes Metals, the country's largest producer of high-grade titanium alloys. His product is used in everything from high-speed magnetic trains to orthopedic joints.
Hero to local charities. Socialite. In short, one of Gotham's golden sons. Until three hours ago, that is...
MUFC SAF
...when Oracle connected him to a secret society called "Mirror House," an organization that auctions off illegal material that once belonged to Gotham's most notorious villains.

CYCLE--
FOLLOW!
STOP THE CAR, RHODES! NOW!
WHUMP
MUFC SAF
BRATTATTAA
NO!

SLAM
MUFC SAF
"NOW WATCH CLOSELY AS I BRING THE DEAD *BACK TO LIFE...*"

...AND...DONE. WILLIAM RHODES IS NOW ALIVE AND WELL, AND ABOUT TO USE HIS CREDIT CARD TO BUY A VINTAGE OF OUR CHOOSING FROM WEST GOTHAM WINES.
ANY RECOMMENDATIONS FOR HIM?
YOU KNOW MY TASTE.
ON SECOND THOUGHT, I'LL CHOOSE. ANY WORD ON THE REDFORD BOY?
SAME. THE REDFORDS MADE THEIR MONEY IN IMPORTS.
MY GUESS? ONE OF THEM FELL IN WITH THIS "DEALER" GUY, LET HIM USE THE FAMILY NAME AND EQUIPMENT TO MOVE AUCTION GOODS.
UNTIL THEY DECIDED NOT TO ANYMORE.
AND THE DEALER DIDN'T LIKE THAT. HENCE THE MAD HATTER TAG.
POOR KID DANA PROBABLY STUMBLED ONTO A STASH BEING KEPT AT HIS HOME FOR AUCTION AT MIRROR HOUSE.

ABOUT MIRROR HOUSE, I'VE BEEN RUNNING ALL KINDS OF A.M.L.'S ON THEIR INVESTMENTS, BUT EVERYTHING IS THREE, EVEN FOUR DUMMY COMPANIES REMOVED. REALLY TRICKY.
BUT.
BUT. I HAVE UNCOVERED A FEW MORE OF ITS CLIENTS.
MAN.
I KNOW. IT READS LIKE A GAZETTE SOCIETY COLUMN. AND THESE ARE ONLY THE ONES I'VE BEEN ABLE TO TRACE.
WHAT ABOUT AN INVITATION TO THE NEXT AUCTION? IS THERE ANYTHING IN RHODES' STUFF?
I'VE FOUND A COUPLE OF ENCRYPTED FILES THAT LOOK SUSPICIOUS. THEY'LL TAKE A LITTLE LONGER TO PRY OPEN.
HOPEFULLY, RHODES' INVITE WILL BE INSIDE ONE, AND ALL YOU'LL HAVE TO DO IS FIX YOUR FACE AND YOU'RE IN.
CAN'T WAIT. I'LL MAKE SURE TO PICK YOU UP A HOUSEWARMING GIFT. MAYBE SOMETHING FOR ME, TOO.
ALFRED WAS AFTER ME THE OTHER DAY FOR NOT MAKING THE PENTHOUSE MORE... "HOMEY."
HAS THIS "ALFRED" PERSON EVER MET YOU?

YOU IF I COME UP WITH ANYTHING.
CIRCUS BLOOD.
THAT SUPPOSED TO MEAN?
COME ON. YOU AND I BOTH KNOW YOU LIKE THE IDEA OF BEING MOBILE, THAT'S ALL. A ROLLING STONE AND ALL THAT STUFF. CIRCUS BLOOD.
YOU'RE A SUPERHERO.
YOU THINK I LIKE THE IDEA OF BEING "MOBILE"?
ARE YOU REALLY ASKING ME THAT WITH ONE LEG OUT MY WINDOW?
FAIR ENOUGH.
AND BABS, THE NEW PLACE...
WHAT? WHAT'S WRONG?
IT LOOKS GOOD ON YOU.

MAN, YOU'D THINK WITH ALL OUR CAPITAL WE COULD AT LEAST BUY SOME COMFORTABLE CHAIRS FOR THE CONFERENCE ROOM.
YOU RUN US INTO THE GROUND YET, TIM?
HARDY HAR. HAPPY NEWS FROM LUCIUS. THE SMART MASK IS HERE. WANT TO TAKE A LOOK?
YOU KIDDING? LUCIUS TALKS ABOUT THE THING LIKE IT'S THE SECOND COMING OF SLICED BREAD.
WELL, BY INTERNATIONAL GEEK STANDARDS, IT IS PRETTY COOL. THESE BEADS HERE, THEY'RE TINY COMPUTERIZED ELECTROMAGNETIC CONDUCTORS.
YOU PROGRAM THEM TO MANIPULATE AND BEND VISIBLE LIGHT.
SO BASICALLY, THE MASK SCULPTS LIGHT...
TO MAKE YOUR FACE LOOK HOWEVER YOU WANT--LIKE WILLIAM RHODES' FACE, FOR EXAMPLE.
ALL PART OF BRUCE'S NEW BATMAN, INCORPORATED "ENHANCEMENTS."
I GUESS THIS MEANS WE'LL BE RETIRING THE OLD BEARD AND WIG TRUNK?
BLASPHEMY, MR. DRAKE. BLASPHEMY.
WHERE YOU HEADED?

"BOARD MEETING OF MY OWN."
COMMISSIONER.
ABOUT *FIFTY POUNDS* OFF. BUT I'LL TAKE IT AS FLATTERY.
LIEUTENANT BULLOCK. WHERE'S THE COMMISSIONER?

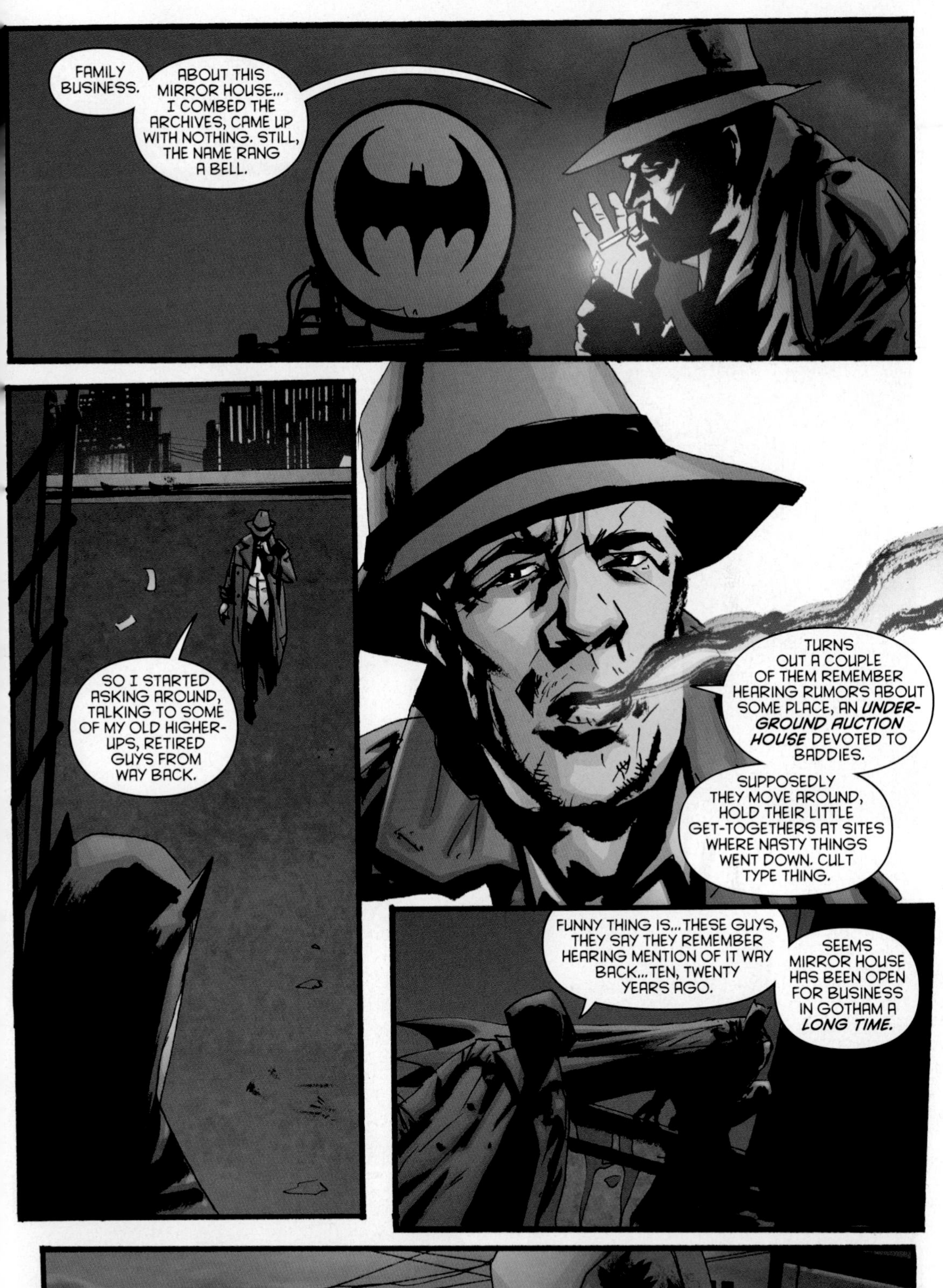
FAMILY BUSINESS.
ABOUT THIS MIRROR HOUSE... I COMBED THE ARCHIVES, CAME UP WITH NOTHING. STILL, THE NAME RANG A BELL.
SO I STARTED ASKING AROUND, TALKING TO SOME OF MY OLD HIGHER-UPS, RETIRED GUYS FROM WAY BACK.
TURNS OUT A COUPLE OF THEM REMEMBER HEARING RUMORS ABOUT SOME PLACE, AN UNDER-GROUND AUCTION HOUSE DEVOTED TO BADDIES.
SUPPOSEDLY THEY MOVE AROUND, HOLD THEIR LITTLE GET-TOGETHERS AT SITES WHERE NASTY THINGS WENT DOWN. CULT TYPE THING.
FUNNY THING IS... THESE GUYS, THEY SAY THEY REMEMBER HEARING MENTION OF IT WAY BACK... TEN, TWENTY YEARS AGO.
SEEMS MIRROR HOUSE HAS BEEN OPEN FOR BUSINESS IN GOTHAM A LONG TIME.

NOT JUST IN GOTHAM.

THE DUMMY COMPANIES THAT FUNNELED MONEY TO BUCK...
...I'VE FOUND RECORDS OF THEM MAKING DEPOSITS IN ACCOUNTS OF POLICE OFFICERS FROM STAR CITY TO METROPOLIS. I SENT THE INFORMATION TO THE COMMISSIONER.
SO WE GOT A PHANTOM AUCTION HOUSE WITH DEEP ROOTS, DEEP POCKETS, AND A LONG REACH.
QUESTION STILL IS, WHO'S BEHIND IT? WHO'S THIS "DEALER" THAT RUNS THE PLACE?
HOLD ON.
WHAT IS IT?
GUESS WHAT I JUST OPENED?
YOUR PERSONAL INVITATION TO TOMORROW'S AUCTION, FROM THE MAN HIMSELF. THE I.P. BELONGS TO A MAN NAMED ETIENNE GUIBORG.
THAT'S AN ALIAS.
77 IRVINGTON STREET
2 AM. TOMORROW NIGHT
APPROPRIATE DRESS REQUIRED
-D.
ETIENNE GUIBORG WAS A PRIEST IN 17th CENTURY FRANCE. HE WAS ACCUSED AND CONVICTED OF SECRETLY PERFORMING BLACK MASSES.
DELIGHTFUL. TALK SOON.
WHAT?
WELL... SPEAK OF THE DEVIL.

This neighborhood, Gramercy Row, used to be a nice place to live.
The earthquake hit it hard, but still, if you'd told me back then that this was what it'd look like today, I would have laughed in your face.
Maybe Barbara is right. Maybe it's the circus blood, but I've lived in Gotham most of my life, and still, I've never gotten over how fast the city can change.
How fast it can turn into a stranger right before your eyes...
HOW'S THE NEW FACE?
IT TICKLES.
NO PROBLEMS, THOUGH?
WHY, TIM?
I RAN AN S.A.T. SCAN, JUST AS AN AFTERTHOUGHT, AND THERE'S A BLACKOUT FIELD IN EFFECT.
MEANING YOU WON'T BE ABLE TO COMMUNICATE WITH ANYONE FROM INSIDE. NO PHONE, NOTHING.

IT SHOULDN'T AFFECT THE MASK IN ANY WAY, BUT EVEN SO...->sstt<-
SHOULDN'T OR WON'T? TIM?
DICK...? DICK, YOU'RE CUT->sstt<-
INVITATION.

GO RIGHT IN, MR. RHODES.
HERE. THEY'VE ALREADY BEGUN.
MAKE SURE YOU OPEN THAT BEFORE YOU ENTER.
Looks like Bullock was right about the location fetish...
It took me a minute to recognize the place. The smell's what gave it away...
...Harbor House. An old banquet hall that once catered to Gotham's upper crust.
47
They were hosting a charity ball when the earthquake hit.
Part of the roof collapsed and sealed the partygoers in.
When the place caught fire, there was no way out.
One half of the crowd trampled the other half, before being burned alive.
Down here, in the banquet hall.

MR. RHODES! YOU'RE JUST IN TIME! WE'RE ABOUT TO BEGIN!
BENJAMIN, THE DOOR, PLEASE...

WELCOME ALL! WELCOME, WELCOME, WELCOME!
CLANK
WHAT A *NIGHT* WE HAVE IN STORE!
FIRST, TO ALL YOU OLD FRIENDS OF MIRROR HOUSE, WELCOME BACK...
42
...AND TO OUR *NEW FRIENDS,* WARMEST SALUTATIONS AND ENTRÉE.
SO HOW ABOUT THIS *LOCATION?*
WONDERFUL, ISN'T IT?
FABULOUS!
YOU CAN STILL FEEL IT! FEEL IT IN THE AIR!

WONDERFUL SPACE, WONDERFUL FRIENDS, WONDERFUL ITEMS TO BID ON... SOON!
FIRST, A QUICK INTRODUCTION FOR OUR NEW FACES IN THE CROWD. NOT THAT I CAN SEE THEM!
HA HA HA!
SO IN CASE YOU'RE WONDERING ABOUT THE MASKS... WHEN IT COMES TO OUR AFFAIRS, WE AT MIRROR HOUSE UNDERSTAND THE NEED FOR BOTH DISCRETION AND EXCLUSIVITY.
WHICH IS WHY THIS ROOM IS COMPLETELY FILLED WITH POISON GAS-- A GAS SPECIALLY CHOSEN FROM GOTHAM'S GRAND HISTORY!
IT'S A REAL VINTAGE, TOO. QUITE POTENT.
IF INGESTED, IT CAUSES ALL SORTS OF DELIGHTFULLY BLACK DELUSIONS BEFORE SPARKING MASSIVE, SUCCESSIVE BRAIN HEMORRHAGES IN ITS VICTIMS!
ALL IN A MATTER OF MINUTES, TOO!
DON'T WORRY THOUG NEW FRIENDS--A ALWAYS, I'VE MA SURE YOUR MASI HAVE BEEN MODIF TO FILTER OUT T PARTICULAR GAS.

NOW, THE PHILOSOPHY OF MIRROR HOUSE IS QUITE SIMPLE. WE BELIEVE, WHOLEHEARTEDLY, THAT EVIL IS HUMANITY'S DIVINE SPARK.
HEAR HEAR!
YES!
SEE, SOME PEOPLE THINK THAT WHAT MAKES US AS A SPECIES DIVINE, WHAT SEPARATES US FROM SOULLESS ANIMALS IS OUR PROPENSITY FOR GOOD.
BOO!
SSSSS!
AND YET, IF I MAY, I'D LIKE TO PROPOSE ANOTHER THEORY.
SPEAK! SPEAK THE TRUTH!
A RETORT, IF YOU WILL... BECAUSE GOODNESS... COMPASSION, GENEROSITY. THESE ARE THINGS THAT DO, IN FACT, OCCUR IN THE WILD, BETWEEN LOWER FORMS OF LIFE. BUT EVIL...
...TRUE MALEVOLENCE, THOUGH...NO. NO, THAT YOU DON'T SEE AMONG THE BIRDS AND THE BEES AND MONKEYS IN THE TREES.
HA HA HA HA HA HA HA HA!

AND SO IT IS IN EVIL, OUR CAPACITY FOR UTTER WICKEDNESS, THAT WE SEE OUR TRUE, DIVINE SELVES REFLECTED MOST CLEARLY.
NOW, AS SOME OF YOU KNOW, MY NAME IS ETIENNE...
...I'VE HAD THE HONOR OF BEING THE DEALER AND AUCTIONEER FOR MIRROR HOUSE FOR MANY YEARS.
I'VE DONE AUCTIONS IN PLACES ALL OVER THE WORLD. BUT THERE'S NOWHERE I LIKE HOLDING AN EVENT MORE THAN GOTHAM CITY.
NOWHERE... NOWHERE IS THE HUMAN SPIRIT MORE VISIBLE THAN THE STREETS OF GOTHAM CITY. YOU CAN FEEL THE CITY FEED ON IT, THE DESIRES OF ITS PEOPLE, THE SHADOWED DREAMS.
WHERE ELSE HOUSES SUCH DARK ANGELS? TWO-FACE. MR. ZSASZ. THE JOKER...
LIVE ON!
47
I tell myself they're just excited by the taboo... by the breaking of the rules...
AND NOW WE BEGIN! OUR FIRST ITEM...
...tell myself that it's like kids daring each other to be bad.

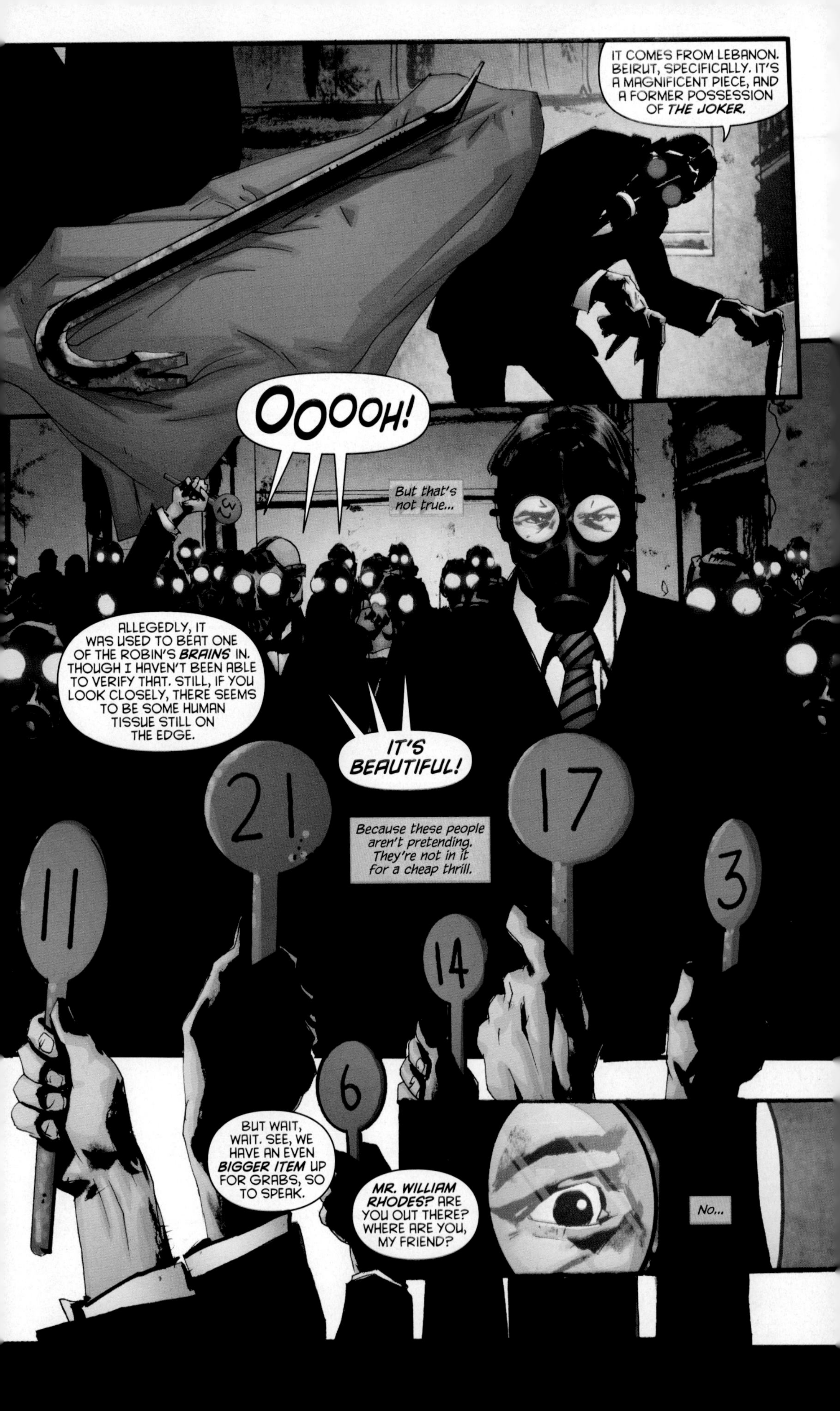
IT COMES FROM LEBANON. BEIRUT, SPECIFICALLY. IT'S A MAGNIFICENT PIECE, AND A FORMER POSSESSION OF *THE JOKER.*
OOOOH!
But that's not true...
ALLEGEDLY, IT WAS USED TO BEAT ONE OF THE ROBIN'S *BRAINS* IN. THOUGH I HAVEN'T BEEN ABLE TO VERIFY THAT. STILL, IF YOU LOOK CLOSELY, THERE SEEMS TO BE SOME HUMAN TISSUE STILL ON THE EDGE.
IT'S BEAUTIFUL!
21
17
Because these people aren't pretending. They're not in it for a cheap thrill.
11
3
14
6
BUT WAIT, WAIT. SEE, WE HAVE AN EVEN *BIGGER ITEM* UP FOR GRABS, SO TO SPEAK.
MR. WILLIAM RHODES? ARE YOU OUT THERE? WHERE ARE YOU, MY FRIEND?
No...

AH, THERE YOU ARE! NUMBER 47. A RICH NUMBER, 47...'47 IS THE YEAR THE AK-47 WAS FIRST PRODUCED. OH, AND THE YEAR OF THE BLACK DAHLIA MURDER IN HOLLYWOOD.
IT'S ALSO THE NUMBER OF SPECIES OF BATS INDIGENOUS TO THIS COUNTRY...
No... this is all wrong...
Something's wrong... can't think.
SEE, FRIENDS, IT'S MY BELIEF THAT MR. RHODES ISN'T WHO HE SAYS HE IS. OH, HIS IDENTIFICATION CHECKED OUT FINE, HIS CREDENTIALS... BUT LOOK CLOSER AND YOU SEE IT'S ALL SMOKE AND MIRRORS.
WHICH IS WHY HIS IS THE ONE MASK I DIDN'T MODIFY.
I IMAGINE YOU MUST BE FEELING THE EFFECTS BY NOW, MR. RHODES?
OR SHOULD I SAY, BATMAN?
THAT'S RIGHT, FRIENDS! I DO BELIEVE THAT WE'RE IN THE COMPANY OF THE BATMAN HIMSELF!
These people, they're not human...
...they're monsters.
I TOLD YOU THIS WAS GOING TO BE A SPECIAL NIGHT! BECAUSE HERE, I GIVE TO YOU, OUR TRUE FIRST ITEM--THE BATMAN! AND THE BEST PART IS, THERE'S NO NEED TO BID! NO, CONSIDER HIM A GIVEAWAY!
SO TAKE HIM! TEAR HIM APART!
Monsters!

AND KEEP HIS BONES FOR YOURSELVES!

SCOTT SNYDER *writer*
JOCK *artist & cover*
DAVID BARON *colors*
JARED K. FLETCHER *letters*

THE BLACK MIRROR

part THREE of THREE

My family had three rules for staying alive on the trapeze. The first was: "Pick a point."
Meaning, pick the point in space you're headed for and never look away, even for a second...

Etienne Guiborg. Commonly known as The Dealer. He runs underground auctions for wealthy Gothamites, auctions devoted to the worship of the city's worst elements.
FRIENDS, I LEAVE MY BELOVED GOTHAM IN THE MORNING. PLEASE, MAKE THIS A NIGHT I CAN SAVOR IN MEMORY UNTIL MY NEXT VISIT!
NOW, TAKE HIM!

All that matters about Guiborg right now, though, is that **he** is the point I've picked.
GRAB HIM!
HIS TEETH! I WANT HIS PRETTY TEETH!
SORRY, FOLKS. I'M AFRAID BIDDING ON THIS ITEM...
...JUST CLOSED.

The gas--I can feel it working on my mind, distorting everything...
GET HIM! GET HIM!
...I can feel myself slipping, losing my grip. Have to stay above them all. Can't fall...
HANG ALL YOU WANT, LITTLE BAT. YOUR PERCH CAN'T HOLD FOREVER...
...I'M COUNTING ON IT.

Have to fight the gas... making my body panic. The tingling in my legs as the endorphins kick in...
Have to stay above them, go higher...
But the feeling is like slipping, like your hands sliding out of the hands holding you.
My family had two more rules, in case the first one didn't work...
...in case you felt yourself giving in to the fear. Sliding...
...losing your grip and starting to fall.

Rule two was "Build yourself a net."
Build a safety net out of plain, simple facts to stop the panic, to steady you.
Facts: My name is Dick Grayson.
I am Gotham City's Batman.
These are the citizens of Gotham. They're just men and women who've gotten a bit too excited by the taboo of all this.
They're not animals...
...not...
...monsters.

GET OFF ME!
But if rule number two wasn't working...
...if you still couldn't shake the fear...and your grip, it wasn't holding...
...my family had a third rule for staying alive...
...which was: "Pray you land somewhere soft."

DICK.
THE DEALER, GUIBORG, HE--
WAIT. SOMETHING'S WRONG WITH...
DICK, TAKE IT EASY.
DICK, THERE'S SOMETHING YOU NEED TO KNOW.
I CAN'T FEEL MY LEGS.
MY GOD, THERE'S NO EASY WAY TO SAY THIS...

NO...NO...
THE MIRROR HOUSE PEOPLE... THEY GOT TO YOU BEFORE TIM DID.
WHEN TIM FOUND YOU, THEY WERE... *EATING YOUR LEGS.*
NO, THIS CAN'T BE HAPPENING.
YOU'RE STILL ALIVE, THOUGH, DICK. YOU'RE INTACT.
WHICH IS ALL I COULD ASK FOR...

BECAUSE IT MEANS THERE'S STILL SOME FOR ME!
DON'T BE LIKE THAT, BABY...

BARBARA, NO, PLEASE!

I JUST WANT A *PIECE* OF YOU.
I LOVE YOU! I'VE *ALWAYS* LOVED YOU!

A LITTLE PIECE...

DICK!
DICK IT'S ME... IT'S--
BABS...
THE GAS... MY GOD, IT WAS SO REAL.
THE TOXIN GUIBORG USED WAS SOMETHING WE HAVEN'T SEEN IN YEARS. WE STILL HAVEN'T FIGURED OUT IF IT'S ONE OF HELFERN'S OR CRANE'S.
WE GAVE YOU A COAGULANT TO STOP THE THREAT OF A STROKE, BUT EVEN SO, IT'S GOING TO TAKE SOME TIME TO WORK ITS WAY THROUGH YOUR SYSTEM.
HOW LONG HAVE I BEEN OUT?
ONLY ABOUT NINE HOURS.

THEN THERE IS NO TIME.
GUIBORG SAID HE WAS LEAVING TOWN IN THE MORNING. THAT MEANS RIGHT NOW.
I NEED TO GET TO THE BUNKER. IF WE PULL UP-- AGGH!
REST IS WHAT YOU NEED. YOU'RE BEATEN TO A PULP. AND THE GAS--
I CAN HANDLE IT. JUST HELP ME ACCESS THE CHARTER WING OF GOTHAM INTERNATIONAL AIRPORT. I CAN DO IT, BUT YOU CAN DO IT FASTER.
IF HE'S LEAVING, HE'S PROBABLY USING THE REDFORD FAMILY PLANE. IT'S A PRIVATE CARGO.
DICK, WE HAVE A BEAD ON THE MONEY. I'M DIGGING IN DEEPER EVERY DAY, EVERY HOUR.
IN A WEEK, WE'LL BE ABLE TO GET THIS GUY WHENEVER AND WHEREVER WE WANT. THERE'S NO RUSH.
NO.

HE NEEDS TO GO DOWN HERE...

"IN GOTHAM. NOW."
MR. GUIBORG. WE HAVE A PROBLEM.
I TOLD YOU, WE'RE USING A DIAMOND CLEARANCE CODE. YOU NEED TO CLARIFY FOR THE TOWER--
SIR, SOMEONE JUST OPENED THE BAY DOOR. WE CAN'T...WE CAN'T CLOSE IT.
NO! MY CARGO! WE'RE LOSING EVERYTHING!
IT'S HIM! BATMAN! LOOK!
TELL DALE TO CLIMB! NOW! THERE'S NO WAY THAT CRAFT WILL BE ABLE TO FOLLOW US PAST 30,000 FEET.
SEE? TOO HIGH FOR A LITTLE BAT.

TURN THE PLANE AROUND, GUIBORG.
THE NATIONAL GUARD HAS FIGHTER JETS EN ROUTE TO ESCORT US BACK TO GOTHAM.
BUT THERE'S NO NEED, LITTLE BAT. YOU AND I, WE ARE GOTHAM. WE FEED ON THE SAME FLESH, THE SAME BLOOD...

NO, IT'S NOT THE GAS AFFECTING YOU, MY LOVE...THIS IS ALL REAL.
FINE. WE'LL DO THIS THE EASY WAY.
HEE, HEE, HEE...
HA HA HA HA HA HA HA HA
OH, YOU SHOULD HAVE STAYED IN YOUR CAVE AND LICKED YOUR WOUNDS, LITTLE BAT.
IN YOUR CAAAVVVE!

SCREEEEE!

OH, LITTLE T...MY DARLING, VE BEEN WAITING SO LONG FOR THIS...
...WAITING FOR YOU TO COME TO ME...
...I LOVE YOU, CAN'T YOU SEE?
I LOVE YOU FOR WHAT YOU GIVE TO GOTHAM... THE MAGNIFICENT INFECTION...

...COME AND LOOK AT ME, LITTLE BAT.
I EAT YOUR MILK...
...I AM THE CHILD AT YOUR NIPPLE.
LOOK IN MY EYES. YOU SEE?
DO YOU SEE?!
WHAT I SEE...

...IS A COMMON CRIMINAL!
A GREEDY OLD MAN...
...WHO SELLS DUSTY PIECES OF JUNK...
...TO RICH PEOPLE WITH TOO MUCH TIME ON THEIR HANDS.
YOU'RE NOT SOME HIGH PRIEST OF EVIL.
OU'RE JUST GERIATRIC...
...BROKEN-DOWN CROOK...
...HOPPED-UP ON VENOM AND SOME OUTDATED VERSION OF DOC LANGSTROM'S MAN-BAT JUICE.
THAT'S RIGHT. I SAW THE MICROSYRINGES.
YOU DON'T OWN GOTHAM CITY.

BUT GOTHAM'S ABOUT TO OWN YOU, FOR A VERY LONG TIME.
MAYBE SOMEDAY... MY LOVE...
...UNTIL THEN...

"THESE, THEY'RE JUST SOME OLD THINGS I FOUND LYING AROUND..."

...LESLIE THOUGHT HAVING A FEW FAMILIAR OBJECTS IN THE ROOM MIGHT HELP, IN CASE THE NIGHTMARE GAS HAS ANY KICK LEFT.
"PSYCHOLOGICAL ANCHORS," AND ALL THAT SHRINKIE-DINK TALK. SO LOOKS LIKE YOU GOT YOUR WISH, ALFIE. THE PENTHOUSE IS NOW GRAYSONIZED.
AS WELL IT SHOULD BE, SIR.
BLUDHAVEN P.D.
COMMENDATION
THE GOTHAM DETACHMENT OF THE COAST GUARD JUST GAVE WORD. THE REDFORD PLANE HAS BEEN RECOVERED FROM THE RIVER.
LET ME GUESS-- NO BODIES INSIDE.
The Flying Graysons
I'M AFRAID NOT, SIR.
MEANWHILE, THE REDFORD BOY, DANA, IS STILL IN THE ICU. -SIGH- ANY OTHER CHEERY NEWS?
The Flying Graysons
THERE IS... ONE MORE MATTER, SIR. WHEN HE DISCOVERED YOU IN THE ALLEY...
...MASTER TIMOTHY FOUND THIS NEARBY.

JUST TOSS IT IN THE RIVER.

AS YOU WISH, SIR.
I'LL TELL YOU, ALFRED, THIS CITY... JUST WHEN YOU THINK YOU'VE SEEN EVERYTHING IT HAS TO THROW AT YOU...

I MEAN, YOU EXPECT THAT KIND OF VICIOUSNESS FROM THE ARKHAM CROWD. BUT THOSE PEOPLE AT MIRROR HOUSE. JUST PLAIN CITIZENS. MOTHERS AND FATHERS...
LATELY IT JUST FEELS LIKE THE CITY IS GETTING MEANER, WILDER. SOMETHING IS CHANGING. SOME NIGHTS I FEEL LIKE I BARELY RECOGNIZE IT ANYMORE.

MAY I REMIND YOU HOW LITTLE SLEEP YOU'VE BEEN GETTING? I TOOK IT UPON MYSELF TO HAVE THE MATTRESS CHANGED AGAIN. SHALL I WAKE YOU FOR A LATE SUPPER, MASTER RICHARD?

MASTER RICHARD?

FRAN CAVIL LA F. 11

These are the questions I get asked the most by people around Gotham...
...and these are my answers.
"You ever shot anyone?" And my answer is, "Too many times."
"You ever been shot?" And my answer is, "Too many times."
POLICE OFFICER CHICAGO POLICE
CHICAGO POLICE DETECTIVE
2209D
DETECTIVE LIEUT GOTHAM CITY POLICE
CAPTAIN GOTHAM CITY POLICE
COMMISSIONER
Happy Father's Day to an Unla... Great Dad. Love, Babs.
And the question I get the most... "How do you leave it all behind when you go home?" My answer to this one is: "You learn to block it out."
GOTHAM CIT
POLICE DEPARTMENT'S WAR ON ORGANIZED CRIME A SUCCESS
Maroni and Falcone Families in Shambles After Series of Bold Convictions.
Clown Prince's Plot to Poison Reservoir Foiled by Intrepid Police Lieutenant
by Vicky Vale
But that's not the truth.
The real truth is that when you've been doing this as long as I have--you don't leave it behind. You can't.
RING RING
Because no matter how good you think you are at drawing a line between work and home, there will always be some cases that stay with you...
...cases that come howling back at you out of the darkness, like phone calls in the middle of the night.
RING RING

RING--
GORDON.
IT'S HARVEY. I'M AT THE AVIARY.
I GOT SOMETHING YOU SHOULD SEE.
I'M LISTENING.
JIM, I THINK IT'S SOMETHING YOU SHOULD SEE. FOR YOURSELF?
SIGH I'LL BE THERE IN FIFTEEN.

SO SOMETIME AROUND SIX IN THE EVENING, JUST AFTER CLOSING, THE CAGES IN THE AVIARY SLEEPING QUARTERS UNLOCKED.
SECURITY
NOW MAYOR HADY, HE'S ALL HOT AND BOTHERED, SEE, BECAUSE HE HAS THESE DIGNITARIES FROM SOME GODFORSAKEN DESERT HOLE VISITING GOTHAM THIS WEEK, AND WHAT'S THEIR FIRST STOP?
THE AVIARY.
HARVEY...IT'S LATE. I GET THE POLITICS, BUT WE GOT A FELONY CRUELTY TO ANIMALS AT BEST HERE.
JUST LISTEN.
THE CAGES IN THIS PLACE ARE ALL AUTOMATED. THEY'RE CONTROLLED BY THE AVIARY'S MAIN COMPUTER SYSTEM.
SECURITY

WHICH MEANS SOME TIME BEFORE CLOSING, OUR GUY SNUCK INTO THE CONTROL ROOM, UNNOTICED, REPROGRAMMED THE CAGES, AND SET ALL THE BIRDS FREE-WILLY TO FLAP AROUND GOTHAM.
A LITTLE PRIVACY, PAL?
SURE THING. EVENING, COMMISSIONER.
DAN.
SO HADY, HE SENDS ME AND MY GUYS DOWN HERE TO LOOK OVER THE SURVEILLANCE FOOTAGE.
SEE IF WE SPY ANYONE SUSPICIOUS COMING OUT OF THE AVIARY TOWARD THE END OF THE DAY. CHOICE ASSIGNMENT, RIGHT?
ANYWAY, I'M LOOKING THROUGH THE LAST HOUR OF TAPE, BARELY PAYING ATTENTION, UNTIL I NOTICE *THIS GUY* EXITING THE MAIN HALL REAL LATE, RIGHT AT CLOSING.
YOU SEEING WHO I'M SEEING, JIM?
JIM?
JIM...

"You want me to put the word out, Jim? Just in case?"
"Thanks, Harvey, no...
"That footage is rough as gravel. You'd be putting the word out on a ghost."

WHO'S HERE?!

SHOW YOURSELF!
JAMES?
JAMES?
JAMES?
...JAMES, WHAT HAVE YOU DONE?
What have you done?
What have you done?
What have you done?

SCREEEEEE
FRAN
CAVIL
LA F.10

GO ON! GET THE HELL OUT OF HERE!
SKELETON CASES
Pt. 1 of 3
SCOTT SNYDER
WRITER
FRANCESCO FRANCAVILLA
ART & COLOR
JARED K. FLETCHER
LETTERS

BARBARA...
DAD?
WE NEED TO TALK.

BAY DIN
YOU KNOW YOU DIDN'T HAVE TO COME ALL THE WAY DOWN, HERE DAD. WHATEVER THIS IS ABOUT, THE LINES IN THERE ARE ALL SECURE ALREADY.
BARBARA...
I FEEL BAD THAT--
IT'S ABOUT YOUR BROTHER.

HE'S BACK?
...IN GOTHAM?
HE MIGHT BE.
WE DON'T KNOW YET.
WELL, WHAT *DO* YOU KNOW WHAT'S THE INTEL?
BARELY ANYTHING. A FEW SECONDS OF SURVEILLANCE FOOTAGE. LO-RES. LESS THAN 500 TVL.
BUT YOU THINK IT'S HIM?
I DON'T KNOW, HONEY...
DAD.
YES.
I THINK IT'S HIM.

ALL RIGHT. I'M GOING.
BARBARA--
I DIDN'T COME HERE TO UPSET YOU. I JUST THOUGHT YOU SHOULD KNOW WE'RE WATCHING FOR HIM.
I'M GLAD YOU'RE WATCHING FOR HIM. I'VE BEEN WATCHING FOR HIM FOR *YEARS.* KEEPING AN EYE OUT IS SOMETHING I'M PRETTY GOOD AT, TOO, AS YOU KNOW.
BUT SEE, EVERY TIME I THINK I HAVE A BEAD ON JAMES, HE DISAPPEARS. BECAUSE HE'S *SMART.* HE'S SMART AND HE'S CUNNING.
I'M UNDER NO ILLUSIONS ABOUT WHAT KIND OF PERSON JAMES IS, BARBARA.

HE'S A KILLER, DAD. A *KILLER.*
AND I KNOW WHAT YOU'RE HINKING, EVEN YOU NEVER SAY T. EVEN IF YOU ON'T ADMIT IT TO YOURSELF. OU'RE THINKING THERE'S NO PROOF.
AND YOU'RE RIGHT. THERE'S NEVER ANY PROOF...HE JUST HAPPENS TO BE THERE WHEN BAD THINGS HAPPEN. BY COINCIDENCE. OVER AND OVER...
JUST PLEASE, LISTEN TO ME, DAD. *PLEASE* HEAR ME THIS TIME. BECAUSE IT'S NOT ABOUT WHY. IT'S NOT ABOUT WHOSE FAULT IT IS...
YOU AND I, WE'VE BEEN THROUGH A LOT OF SCARY STUFF IN OUR LIVES. *TERRIFYING* STUFF. BUT LET ME TELL YOU, THERE ARE ONLY A FEW THINGS I HAVE NIGHTMARES ABOUT.
ONE IS THAT DOOR. THAT DOOR OPENING AND THE GUN...
AND ANOTHER IS JAMES. JAMES, STARING AT ME ACROSS THE LAWN, HOLDING BESS'S KEYCHAIN IN HIS HAND. TURNING IT OVER AND OVER. SMILING AT ME...
I'M SORRY. I HAVE TO GO.
BARBARA...

ANYTHING I CAN GET YOU, COMMISSIONER?
COMMISSIONER?
WHAT? OH...
...I'M SORRY. CAN YOU GIVE ME A MINUTE?
I THINK JUST A COFFEE.
BLACK, NO SUGAR...

HI, DAD.
BEEN A WHILE.
Bay
DINER
2927 24th ST.
GOTHAM CITY
Serving Poached Eggs
Monday thru Friday
At 11 am
Saturday & Sunday
At 10 am
SKELETON CASES
part 2 of 3
BATMAN CREATED by
BOB KANE
Senior discount Every Day
WRITER
SCOTT SNYDER.......... 3.99
ARTIST & COLORS
FRANCESCO FRANCAVILLA..... 3.99
LETTERS
JARED K. FLETCHER.......... 3.99
Dessert is on the house!
SNYDER S.10
FRANCAVILLA '10

THE SILVER BOX DINER. GOTHAM HARBOR.
THREE NIGHTS AGO...
JAMES...?
DAD. I'M NOT HERE TO UPSET YOU OR BARBARA.
YOU JUST STOPPED BY TO FREE SOME POOR, CAPTIVE BIRDS, OF COURSE.
I'M SORRY, I DON'T KNOW WHAT THAT MEANS.

I SAW YOU ON CAMERA, JAMES. AT THE AVIARY.
I WAS AT THE AVIARY. I ALWAYS GO THERE WHEN I'M IN TOWN. I HAVE GOOD MEMORIES.
YOU KNOW WHAT? I'M DONE.
I CAN'T DO THIS ANYMORE. LOVE YOU, JAMES, I ALWAYS WILL. BUT I CAN'T...
DAD, I'M ONLY SKING YOU FOR TWO NUTES. TWO MINUTES D THEN I'LL LEAVE AND WON'T BOTHER YOU AGAIN. I PROMISE.
PLEASE.
WHAT'S THAT ON YOUR SHIRT?

IT'S BLOOD, DAD. I KILLED A WAITRESS WHILE YOU WERE TALKING TO BARBARA. HER HEAD IS STUFFED IN THE TOILET OF THE MEN'S ROOM.
IT'S JUS KETCHU SEE?
I'M SORRY.

I WAS TRYING TO MAKE A JOKE...I'M NOT GOOD AT HUMOR. THAT'S PART OF IT. I'M SORRY.
TWO MINUTES. THEN I'M GONE.

ALL RIGHT, JAMES. HERE'S WHAT'S GOING TO HAPPEN--I'M GOING TO SIT HERE AND DRINK MY COFFEE.
WHEN I'M DONE, WE'RE DONE.
FAIR ENOUGH. THANK YOU.
I CAME TO SAY THAT...I KNOW HOW MUCH PAIN I'VE CAUSED YOU OVER THE YEARS. I DO. MOM, TOO. SARAH. BARBARA. I'M HERE TO SAY... I'M SORRY.
YOU'RE SORRY.
I'M NOT GOING TO PRETEND I'M A GOOD PERSON. HAVE I HURT PEOPLE? YES. HAVE I DONE BAD THINGS--?
BAD THINGS? YOU PRACTICALLY TORTURED THOSE GUYS TO DEATH, JAMES, AND WHY? BECAUSE THEY MADE FUN OF YOU A LITTLE? AND WHAT ABOUT ALL THE FOLKS AT THE WAYNE J.R.C. YOU ALMOST BURNED ALIVE, HUH?
BAD THINGS... JESUS, WHAT ABOUT BESS KELLER, BACK WHEN YOU WERE THIS HIGH--
I NEVER HURT BESS.

YEAH, WELL, BARBARA THINKS DIFFERENT. YOU KNOW, SHE THINKS YOU'RE A KILLER. A MURDERER. AND NOT JUST BESS, EITHER. TO HEAR HER OPINION... I CAN'T EVEN...
BARBARA HAS A LOT OF OPINIONS OF ME. AGAIN, I'M NOT A GOOD MAN, DAD. BUT I'M NOT A KILLER. *I'VE NEVER KILLED ANYONE.*
LOOK, I TOLD YOU, I'M NOT HERE TO UPSET YOU. I'M HERE TO TELL YOU I'M SORRY.
BUT I'M ALSO HERE TO ASK YOU SOME-THING...
...AFTER I LEFT GOTHAM LAST TIME, I TRAVELED AROUND, ALL OVER. I FIGURED MAYBE IT WAS THIS PLACE...I THOUGHT MAYBE IF I GOT AWAY FROM GOTHAM, I'D FINALLY STOP BEING...BEING THE WAY I AM.
BUT EVERYWHER I WENT, I GOT INTO TROUBLE.
THEN, ABOUT A YEAR AGO, I WAS IN TEXAS. NEAR HOUSTON. I WAS DOING MY WASH IN THIS LAUNDROMAT AND SOME GOOD OL' BOYS CAME IN, ALL DRUNK.
HASSLING ME, CALLING ME A BU AND TELLING ME T GET LOST AND ALL T ONE OF THEM, HE S IN MY LAUNDRY... THOUGHT THAT WAS FUNNY.
I JUST TOOK IT, TOO. BECAUSE I WAS THINKING TO MYSELF, THIS IS A TEST. AND IF I CAN NOT DO WHAT I NORMALLY DO...IF I CAN JUST HOLD IT TOGETHER...
WHAT DID YOU DO, JAMES...?

BUT EVEN AS I WAS THINKING THIS, DAD, I WAS MEMORIZING THE LICENSE PLATE ON THEIR CAR. THINKING HOW FUN IT WAS GOING TO BE TO HURT THEM. HURT THEIR GIRLFRIENDS OR WIVES. THEIR MOTHERS. HECK, THEIR PETS...
WHAT DID YOU *DO?*
...AND THAT NIGHT, I FOUND THE ADDRESS OF THE GUY WHO SPIT ON MY CLOTHES, AND I WENT TO HIS HOUSE, AND...
JAMES--
I DIDN'T DO ANYTHING. I DIDN'T HURT THAT MAN IN HOUSTON. I STOPPED MYSELF.
THE NEXT MORNING, I CHECKED MYSELF INTO HOUSTON GENERAL'S PSYCH CENTER. I WAS JUST SO TIRED, DAD. TIRED OF BEING WHO I WAS.
BUT THEN THIS AMAZING THING, THIS ***MIRACLE*** HAPPENED... BECAUSE I MET GOOD DOCTORS THERE. REALLY GOOD DOCTORS. AN EXPERT IN PSYCHO-PATHOLOGY. AND THAT WAS THE START FOR ME.
THE START OF WHAT?
OF THIS, DAD. OF GETTING BETTER. BECAUSE HERE IS WHAT I'VE LEARNED.
I AM A PSYCHOPATH.

JAMES--
NO. IT'S NOT SOME INSULT. I UNDERSTAND THIS NOW.
IT'S A CLINICAL DIAGNOSIS. THE AMYGDALA, DAD-- IT'S THE PART OF THE BRAIN THAT HELPS WITH SOCIALIZATION.
IT'S WHAT ALLOWS PEOPLE TO INTERPRET SIGNALS FROM THE OUTSIDE WORLD CORRECTLY. IN PEOPLE LIKE ME, THOUGH, IT UNDER-PRODUCES.
NOW WHETHER I WAS BORN THIS WAY, OR THE FALL CAUSED IT, OR SOMETHING ELSE... IT DOESN'T MATTER.
WHAT MATTERS IS THESE DOCTORS IN HOUSTON, THEY GOT ME INTO THIS...CLINICAL TRIAL.
A DRUG TRIAL?
IT'S CALLED *DIAXAMYNE.* IT STIMULATES THE AMYGDALA TO PRODUCE MORE PEPTIDES. WHICH ALLOWS SOMEONE LIKE ME TO RECEIVE SIGNALS A LITTLE BETTER--SIGNALS FROM THE OUTSIDE WORLD.
IS IT A CURE FOR A.S.P.D.? NO. BUT IT'S A START.
THE POINT IS, I STARTED TAKING THIS NINE MONTHS AGO. AND AFTER SOME FITS AND STARTS, I'VE FOUND SOME CALM.
DO I HAVE BAD THOUGHTS SOME-TIMES? DO I GET... ANGRY? SOMETIMES. BUT I'M TRYING, DAD. THAT'S WHAT I CAME TO TELL YOU. AND I WANT TO HELP PEOPLE... PEOPLE LIKE ME.
JAMES, WHAT ARE YOU ASKING FOR?

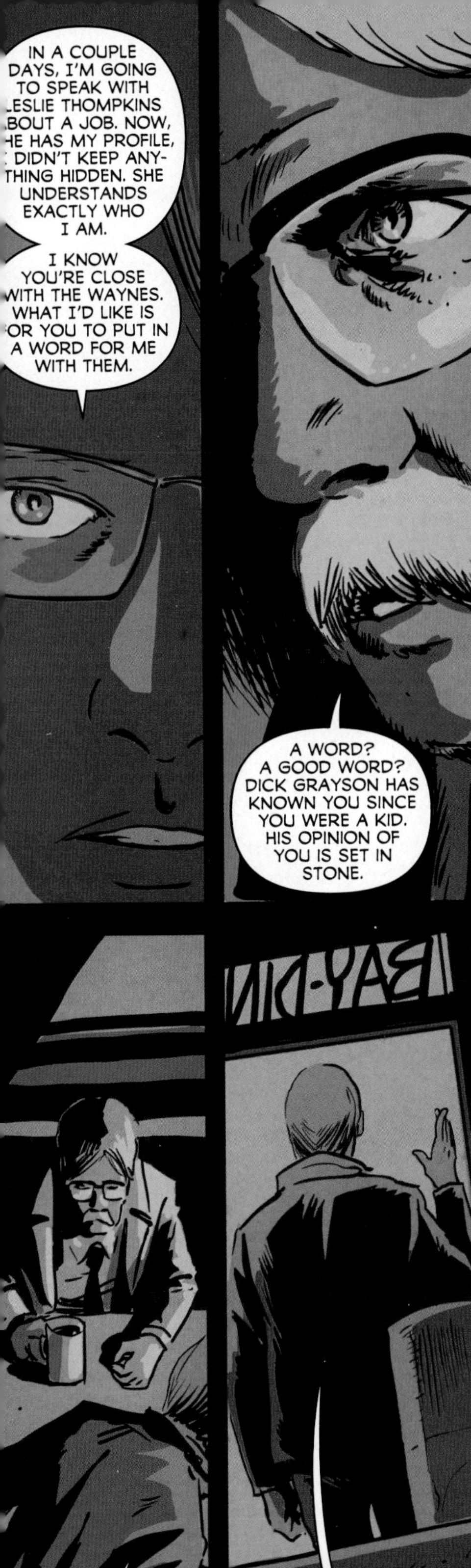
IN A COUPLE DAYS, I'M GOING TO SPEAK WITH ESLIE THOMPKINS BOUT A JOB. NOW, HE HAS MY PROFILE, DIDN'T KEEP ANY-THING HIDDEN. SHE UNDERSTANDS EXACTLY WHO I AM.
I KNOW YOU'RE CLOSE WITH THE WAYNES. WHAT I'D LIKE IS OR YOU TO PUT IN A WORD FOR ME WITH THEM.
A WORD? A GOOD WORD? DICK GRAYSON HAS KNOWN YOU SINCE YOU WERE A KID. HIS OPINION OF YOU IS SET IN STONE.

BUT HE RESPECTS YOU. LOOK, I'M NOT ASKING YOU TO TELL HIM I'M A GOOD PERSON. ALL I'M ASKING IS FOR YOU TO REQUEST THAT HE DOESN'T PUT IN A *BAD* WORD, OR BLOCK ME FROM APPLYING.
I'M ASKING YOU TO DO NOTHING. AND TO TELL HIM TO DO NOTHING. THAT'S IT.

I SHOULD LEAVE. BUT I'M STAYING AT THE RIVERVIEW OARDING HOUSE. ROOM 7. IT'S GOOD TO SEE YOU, DAD.
YOUR COFFEE'S GETTING COLD.

SKELETON CASES pt.3
BATMAN created by BOB KANE
SCOTT SNYDER Story
FRANCESCO FRANCAVILLA ART, COVER, & COLORS
LETTERS JARED K. FLETCHER

"YOU'RE FOOLING YOURSELF AGAIN.
"YOU KNOW IT, AND I KNOW IT. AND IT'S A DANGEROUS HOLE YOU'RE HEADED DOWN.
OTHAM CITY
DEPARTMENT OF
NMENTAL PROTECTION
WATER MANAGEMENT
PLANT NO.5
"BECAUSE YOU CAN PRETEND THE POISON'S GONE.
"PRETEND IT'S BEEN CLEANED OUT.
"BUT DEEP DOWN YOU AND I KNOW IT'S STILL THERE CIRCULATING THROUGH."
GOTHAM SHIPYARD.
NOW.
ARE YOU LISTENING TO ME, BATMAN? I'M SAYING THAT THE GAS THE DEALER USED ON YOU WAS POWERFUL STUFF.

I'M FINE, RED ROBIN. BESIDES... YOU'RE HERE NOW.
YOU'RE NOT FINE. AND WITH OR WITHOUT ME, YOU SHOULDN'T BE OUT ON PATROL YE--
SSHH HERE THEY COME.
TARGET DISTANCE...
62'
51'
54'
55'
45'
THERE. IN THAT CAGE. THE HARPY EAGLE THAT ESCAPED FROM THE AVIARY.
POACHERS, HUH? AND THEY DON'T KNOW IT'S STATE MANDATE FOR ANIMALS IN CAPTIVITY TO BE IMPLANTED WITH SUBCUTANEOUS TRACERS?
THEY CUT THE TRACER OUT THIS MORNING-- GAVE IT TO SOME KID TO RUN AROUND THE CITY WITH.
LUCKILY, I'D ALREADY PLANTED ONE OF LUCIUS' BABIES ON THEIR CAR.
RECOGNITION ...
NO IDEA WHO THEY WORK FOR YET?
searching...
found: HARPY EAGLE
NOPE. BUT BE CAREFUL, RED ROBIN. THEY'RE WEARING SUN-GLASSES AT NIGHT. WHICH MEANS THEY'RE VERY, VERY COOL.

I can joke all I want.
I know that Tim's right.
The toxin is still in me.
I can feel it moving through
my veins, my arteries.
It's like a whisper--like a
voice rising from the dark.

Not loud anymore, but soft.

CREW ONLY
FRAN GAVIL LAF.11
Something I can fend off...

...something
I have to fight...

COMING FOR YOU DICKIE
WHAT THE?
GOING TO EAAAT YOU UP!
Eat you up til there's nothin left
BATMAN, LOOK OUT!
Sloppy. Shake it off, Dick.

See through it.
Your mind is a shark.
A shark swim--
COMinG..
Coming
To
EAt you!
No...that can't...
Eat you uP DICKiE!!!
EAT YOU!
EAT YOU!
EAT YOU!!

I GOT YOU.
YOU OKAY?
THERE WAS A... I SAW...
WHAT? YOU SAW WHAT?
NOTHING.
I MEAN, YEAH, I'M ALL RIGHT.
I DOUBT THAT, BUT EITHER WAY. COME ON, I WANT TO SHOW YOU SOMETHING.

WOW.
A ROSADA IGUANA. A GOLD-BACKED TARANTULA. EVERY-THING IN THIS ROOM IS HIGHLY ENDANGERED.
WHO DO YOU THINK--YAKUZA?
I THOUGHT SO AT FIRST, BECAUSE OF THE FIGHTING STYLE, BUT THE TATTOOS DON'T LOOK LIKE TRADITIONAL IREZUMI, SEE?
NOT TO MENTION THEY ALL SEEM TO HAVE A COMPLETE SET OF FINGERS.
NO, I THINK THIS IS SOMEONE NEW.
SOMEONE WE HAVEN'T SEEN BEFORE.

"NOT SOMEONE COME BACK TO GET US FROM BEFORE..."
MISSING BOY FOUND DEAD
PETER PAN STRIKES AGAIN?
SCOTT SNYDER FRANCESCO FRANCAVILLA
MISSING

FRAN CAVIL LA F. 10

People call me old-fashioned. The younger guys on the force, they bust my chops because I don't speak their language. Harvey Bullock, dinosaur...
...because, nope, I didn't see that show last night, where they all prance around and belt out awful covers and vote each other into the damn ocean or whatnot.
I like my stuff classic. Hell, I'm only up here now because it's the only place I can sometimes catch my favorite radio station, a rinky-dink AM that plays the oldies. The real ones.
See, the younger guys don't get it yet. Because when you live and work in a place like Gotham, you've got to have your anchors. The things you like, things you hold on to.
Because the city... it keeps changing every day. Every hour, throwing curveballs at you.
You turn around and you got a new Batman standing on your roof. You got new psychos and freaks, like this Dealer guy, trying to gas and rip Batman apart...
AM
FM

And Jim Gordon... just last week his kid, James Jr., comes back after God knows how long.
James was always a bad eed, spooky as they come. w he comes back and tells oor Jim he's changed...he's aking meds that help him keep himself in check...
That's what I mean. What this city will throw at you...you got to have your things. Your steadies.
Things you build a home out of, a nest for your--
Then again, maybe you just use your head...
...and you make your home somewhere else. Somewhere far, far away.

If you're thinking about visiting Gotham City, all the travel guides give the same piece of advice--
"Visit in the winter."
They all talk about the snow, how it makes the city look "fresh" and "bright" and "new."
CLOSED BRIDGE -KEEP OUT-
Read between the lines and it's clear that what they're saying is you should visit Gotham when the real city is covered up.
My name is Jim Gordon. And I've never liked winter in Gotham.
The snow always makes me restless--the way it buries everything.
WAYNE IND.
All I can think about is the footprint in the alley filling with white. The cotton thread on the windowsill loosening with every icy drip. Clues lost.

ZOOM 10X
CHEAP EATS
CIGARS
They come at me in winter, the **unsolved** ones. The ones I couldn't crack.
LIQUORS
BEERS
OPEN
CLOSED
62'
54'
ACQUIRING TARGET...
ZOOM 12X
If you're wondering if there's a worst one...
55'
CLOSED
LIQUORS
BEERS
...a case from long ago that digs at me more than any other on nights like these...
TARGET ACQUIRED.
ZOOMING IN...
ZOOM 16X
...I can say without hesitation that yes, there is.
FACIAL RECOGNITION SEARCH IN PROGRESS...
searching...
ZOOM 18X
But tonight, I'm going to close the book on it, ***once and for all.***
TARGET IDENTIFIED
BLOUNT, Roy M.
FF

FIND ANYTHING, *LIEUTENANT GORDON?*
SORRY, COMMISSIONER McKEEVER, NOT AN ACCESS POINT IN SIGHT.
SPACE WARS
AND THE ROOF?
G.C.
I HAD OFFICER BULLOCK CHECK IT BACK TO FRONT. NOTHING TO HANG A ROPE OFF ANYWHERE.
NOTHING. PERFECT. *SIGH* YOU KNOW WHAT THE GAZETTE IS CALLING HIM NOW, JIM? THE ***"PETER PAN KILLER."***
HALF THE CITY'S READY TO BELIEVE IT, TOO. HELL, WHY NOT? GUY SNEAKS IN THROUGH KIDS' BEDROOM WINDOWS IN THE MIDDLE OF THE NIGHT, STEALS THEM FROM THEIR BEDS.
SEVEN KIDS DEAD SINCE SUMMER, NOW AN EIGHTH MISSING, AND WE'VE GOT NO CLUES, NO WITNESSES. JUST THE DAMN OPEN WINDOW HE SLITHERS THROUGH.
I BELIEVE THE WINDOW'S A MISLEAD, SIR.
IT'S THE KIND OF CATCHY DETAIL HE KNOWS SOMEONE ON THE FORCE WILL LEAK TO THE PRESS FOR A FEW BUCKS.

MEANWHILE, THE GUY COMES THROUGH THE FRONT DOOR.
THE PAPERS PRINT IT, WARNING ABOUT THE PETER PAN KILLER WHO SNEAKS IN THROUGH THE WINDOWS, SO EVERYONE BUYS NEW WINDOW LOCKS.
LIEUTENANT? PHONE CALL FOR YOU. IT'S YOUR WIFE.
OU'RE SURE YOU CAN'T TICK AROUND HIS WEEKEND, JIM?
WE COULD USE YOU AT THE PRESS CONFERENCE.
I'M SORRY, COMMISSIONER. BUT SARAH AND I HAVE BEEN PLANNING THIS TRIP FOR MONTHS. THE HOUSE IS PAID UP.
WE'LL REIMBURSE YOU. HELL, I'LL REIMBURSE YOU. I GOT MY DAMN CHECKBOOK IN MY COAT.
SARAH?
IT'S ME, JIM.
...BARBARA?
I'M SORRY. I TOLD THE MAN "EX-WIFE," BUT HE MUST HAVE MISHEARD ME. I DIDN'T MEAN TO BOTHER YOU IF YOU'RE ON SITE.
IT'S ALL RIGHT. IS EVERYTHING OKAY?
YES. I MEAN, I JUST WANTED TO SAY THANK YOU...FOR TAKING JAMES ALONG THIS WEEKEND.
HE'S LOOKING FORWARD TO IT. HE SEEMS TO BE RATHER...
IT'S HARD TO TELL.

HOW HAS HE BEEN?
⊰SIGH⊱ THE SAME. I GOT CALLED INTO SCHOOL AGAIN. A KID WHO WAS BULLYING HIM, SOME FOOTBALL PLAYER, ATE SOMETHING THAT LANDED HIM IN THE HOSPITAL.
THEY DON'T HAVE ANY PROOF, OF COURSE, THEY JUST WANTED TO SEE WHAT I THOUGHT ABOUT THE NOTION.
I BROUGHT HIM TO ANOTHER DOCTOR.
AND?
AND IT'S NOT AUTISM.
WHAT DO YOU MEAN? WHAT IS IT THEN?
HE WANTS TO GIVE JAMES A TEST. HE WANTS TO GIVE HIM A P.C.L.
A P.C.L.? THAT'S ABSURD, BARB. THEY GIVE THAT OUT AT ARKHAM. IT GAUGES PSYCHO-PATHOLOGY.
I KNOW THAT, JIM. DON'T YOU THINK I KNOW THAT? THE THINGS HE SAYS SOMETIMES, THOUGH... YOU NEVER KNOW EXACTLY WHAT HE MEANS, BUT THERE'S SOMETHING COLD IN--
JIM?
JIM, I NEED YOU OVER HERE.
BARB, LISTEN, WE'LL TAKE HIM TO ANOTHER DOCTOR. WE'LL GET ANOTHER OPINION, OKAY? I HAVE TO GO. I'M WORKING A TOUGH CASE...

The Peter Pan case. Fifteen years ago, over the course of eight months, eight children went missing from their beds.
CHEAP EATS
Eventually, one by one, their bodies turned up in the city dump. They'd been drugged unconscious with **ether**... mutilated.
As a cop, I deal with the human capacity for evil every day.
It's a fact. It exists in people. People like **Roy Blount.**
You might not see it at first glance. Because on the surface, he's just a quiet man who owns a small cleaning business.
GOTHAM GAZ
Sure, he did some time at Blackgate for **arson,** but he was just a stupid kid playing with matches. He didn't mean to set that fire.
Hell, no one was even hurt, except him. Burned up his whole left side. Either way, look at him, he paid his dues. He's just trying to get his life back on track is all. He's an earnest, stand-up guy.
But look closer, look right when I tell you, and you'll see it too, the **real** Roy beneath the surface.
He has been out of jail a week, and I've watched him every night.
Because when you've been a cop as long as I have, you get good at seeing it in people, that **dark spark** of something... something beneath.

SOB BUT HE NEVER CRIES, JIM. WHAT KIND OF A BABY NEVER CRIES?
Right now, at this very moment, my son James is staying in a boarding house across town.
He's waiting for me to see him. He claims he's on a medication that has made him into a better person than he used to be...
So the real question is--what do I see when I look at my son?
There was never any question that something was different about James... that something was wrong.
I JUST WANTED TO SEE WHERE IT KEEPS ITS EGGS.
But wrong how? Wrong why? Was it the fall that did it? The trauma? Was it me? Some nights, when he was little, I'd look at him and think it was the city, this twisted city that was twisting him...
And I'd scoop him up and hold him and look for somewhere I could take him...
READY, DAD!
...somehere we could go. Somewhere safe where he'd stay small and innocent forever. But deep down I knew it...
YOU TAKE THAT CRAP OFF YOUR FACE RIGHT NOW!
JIM, STOP. HE DOESN'T UNDERSTAND.

...I knew there was nowhere to go.
AND, WE'RE HERE.
JAMES, YOUR ROOM IS THE SECOND DOOR ON YOUR RIGHT. MAKE YOURSELF AT HOME.
FF-O22O11
THANKS, MRS. GORDON.
HOW MANY TIMES DO I HAVE TO TELL YOU, SILLY? CALL ME SARAH!
BESS!
YOU GOT THE BOX?
RIGHT HERE. YOU GOT THE KEY?
WHAT'S THAT?
OH, HEY, JAMES. THIS IS BESS. SHE LIVES JUST DOWN THE WAY.
BESS, MY STEPBROTHER, JAMES.
FRAN GAVIL LAF.11

WOW! ≥HAHA≤ THOSE ARE SOME SERIOUS SPACE GOGGLES.
SUN HITS THEM THE WRONG WAY AND YOU COULD FRY SOMEONE. BE CAREFUL!
EXCUSE ME?

DON'T LISTEN TO HER. SHE'S JUST TEASING YOU.

OH. I GET IT. BECAUSE OF MY GLASSES. MEANING, THE LENSES COULD FOCUS THE SUNLIGHT TO CREATE A HOTSPOT. THAT'S... FUNNY.
YOU WERE ASKING ABO THIS, THOUG

IT'S A SCIENCE KIT. BESS AND I BOUGHT IT TOGETHER A COUPLE YEARS AGO. WE SHARE IT. I KEEP THE BOX, SHE KEEPS THE KEY. SO WE CAN ONLY USE IT WHEN WE'RE TOGETHER.
VOILA.

CAN I SEE IT?
SURE, IT'S HEAVY THOUGH. HERE.

SO, TELL ME ABOUT THE OLDER BOYS, BABS.
TELL YOU WHAT?
OH COME ON, YOU SKIP TWO GRADES AND...WHAT THE--

WHAT THE HELL ARE YOU *DOING?*

HE ALMOST BROKE THE LOCK. LOOK AT THIS! YOU LITTLE TWERP.
WHY WOULD YOU DO THAT, JAMES?
Science Kit

I WAS TRYING TO OPEN IT FOR YOU, BARBARA. BUT THE LOCK IS TRICKY.
BUT... WHO SAID I WANTED IT OPENED?
I'M SORRY. I JUST FIGURED, THAT WAY, IF BESS EVER *WENT AWAY,* YOU'D STILL BE ABLE TO USE IT YOURSELF.

WENT AWAY? WHAT ARE YOU TALKING ABOUT?
WHY WOULD SHE EVER GO AWAY, JAMES?

I MEANT *MOVED* AWAY. WHAT IF HER FAMILY MOVED SOMEDAY.

UGH COME ON, BABS...LET'S GO.
JEEZ, AND I THOUGHT *MY* BROTHER WAS CREEPY.

YOU CAN PLAY WITH THEM IF YOU WANT, JAMES.
THAT'S OKAY, MRS. GORDON. I CAN MAKE MY OWN FUN.
There. There it is. You see it? He's going to kill someone tonight.

There in Roy's eyes.
To everyone else, he's just a man walking down a snowy alley.
But you saw it. It's all still there underneath.
The real Roy beneath this one. The predator. The killer.
No, that Roy, the one beneath, he hasn't gone anywhere...
ETHER

RING RING
"GORDON RESIDENCE..."
"WHAT? NO, NO...BESS LEFT HOURS AGO."
"OKAY. CALM DOWN. I'LL WALK THE PATH RIGHT NOW. I'LL GET SOMEONE OUT ON THE WATER, TOO...I KNOW, I KNOW IT EMPTIES OUT INTO THE OCEAN, BOB."
"WE'LL FIND HER."
FRANCAVILLA F.11

ANYTHING?
NOT YET. THE OTHERS ARE STILL LOOKING.

JIM? WE'RE DOUBLING BACK. OVER.
GOT IT. WE SHOULD HAVE MORE EYES UP HERE ANY MINUTE. OVER.
TELL HIM, HONEY.

TELL ME WHAT?
I SAW SOMETHING IN JAMES'S HAND, DAD.

THERE WAS SOMETHING IN IT, AND I THINK IT WAS BESS'S KEYCHAIN.

HER KEYCHAIN? WHAT ARE YOU SAYING, BARBARA?
I'M SAYING...

...I THINK HE *DID* SO THING TO H DADDY...

THINK IT
S HIM."
You scratch the surface and the evidence is there. It adds up. Like with Roy.
See, before he caused that mysterious fire, e already had a record as a sex offender.
His weren't big offenses, nothing huge. But all of them involved children.
Still, all that got hidden during Roy's time in Blackgate. Because by a glitch, his record as a sex offender was allowed to expire during his incarceration.
Look deeper and you'll find another clue: because that burn on old Roy's arm and neck, it's a flash burn.
511
YOU KNOW, I USED TO READ PETER PAN TO MY DAUGHTER WHEN SHE WAS A LITTLE GIRL. YOU REMEMBER HOW IT ENDS, ROY? I'LL TELL YOU...

...PETER PAN, HE COMES BACK TO WENDY'S HOUSE AFTER ALL THOSE YEARS...
511
he kind of thing that happens when a highly combustible fluid ignites. Like ether. Like if you had ether on you, and you were smoking a igarette, and you weren't careful...
you'd go up like a flare, and then you'd get caught, and then you'd get sent away.
And see, then, if someone like me, they happened to notice that right around the time you got sent away, the Peter Pan killings stopped... they'd find another clue, Roy.
...AND HE FINDS THE WINDOW LOCKED.
Because with a little cross-referencing, they'd see that all the families with kids that disappeared, all of them used your cleaning business at one time or another.
And if you, Roy, cleaned their houses, then it'd stand to reason you'd have ample opportunity to leave the door unlatched or make a key to fit... if you wanted. And then, Roy...

...it would be game over.
JAMES. I NEED TO SPEAK WITH YOU.
COME IN.
DID YOU FIN HER?
NO... NO, WE DIDN'T.
I'M SORRY TO HEAR THAT.
WHAT IS THAT YOU'RE DOING?
I'M JUST DOING AN EXPERIMENT, IS ALL.
HOW DID YOU OPEN THE CASE, JAMES?
WHAT DO YOU MEAN, DAD? I USED THIS KNIFE.
A PLAIN, OLD KNIFE.
"I KNOW WHO YOU ARE..."

...YOU'RE... YOU'RE JIM GORDON.

SUPER-COP, *HEH.* YOU WERE ALWAYS RIGHT BEHIND ME.

SWING YOURSELF TOWARD THE LEDGE, BLOUNT! I CAN'T HOLD YOU.

YOU WANT A CONFESSION, GORDON?
ONE DAY BACK THEN, I DECIDED HELL, YOU WERE OUT TO GET ME, WHY NOT COME AFTER YOU, TOO?

SO THE SUMMER BEFORE MY ACCIDENT, I ***DID*** COME AFTER YOU...

...I FOLLOWED YOU UP TO THAT SUMMER HOUSE OF YOURS...
...AND I CAME FOR YOUR BOY...

"...I CAME FOR JAMES."
WHAT DID YOU DO, JAMES?
WHAT DID YOU DO?
WHAT DO YOU MEAN, DAD?
I DIDN'T DO ANYTHING, DAD! I WAS HERE THE WHOLE TIME!
NO MORE LIES...

"...TELL ME THE *TRUTH!*"
SO ONE DAY ≥COUGH≤...I WAITED OUTSIDE 'TIL YOUR OLD LADY LEFT JAMES ALONE FOR A SECOND...

...AND I WALKED UP TO HIM, AND I HAD A WHOLE STORY CONCOCTED, HOW I WAS LOST, HOW I HAD TOYS IN MY CAR...

TELL ME THE TRUTH, DAMMIT!
"...HE LOOKED UP AT ME. AND..."

...HE SMILED AND HE SAID, "I KNOW WHO YOU ARE"...AND THE LOOK HE GAVE ME, IT SENT CHILLS UP MY BACK. ***ME...***

YOU'RE LYING...
LET GO, JIM!

IT WAS ***YOU,*** WASN'T IT, ROY?! ***YOU KILLED BESS!*** YOU!
LET GO, COMMISSIONER.

YOU CAN LET GO NOW, COMMISSIONER. IT'S OVER.
But how could it be over when we never found Bess? Or the keychain?
Or any evidence connecting James to her disappearance?
YOU SHOULD GO. I CAN HEAR THEM COMING.
I HEARD THEM TWO AND A HALF MINUTES AGO.
ONE THING. I WAS ABLE TO ACCESS THE SAT-COM FEED YOU REQUESTED. OF THE AVIARY.
AND?

"AND I DON'T KNOW WHO YOU WERE EXPECTING TO SEE OPEN HOSE *BIRD CAGES,* BUT IT WAS JUST A COUPLE SKATER PUNKS. COULDN'T HAVE BEEN MORE THAN THIRTEEN YEARS OLD...
"SO IS THAT GOOD NEWS, COMMISSIONER?"
"FUNNY THING IS, I'M NOT SURE ANYMORE."
G.C.P.D
"IS ANY OF THIS PART OF SOMETHING I SHOULD KNOW ABOUT?"
"JUST AN OLD CASE...
"...SOMETHING THAT DIGS AT ME, ON NIGHTS LIKE THESE."
LOST BOYS
SCOTT SNYDER writer
FRANCESCO FRANCAVILLA artist
JARED K. FLETCHER LETTERS
SNYDER S.11 FRANCAVILLA F.11

"GOTHAM GLOBAL MODERN BANK OCCUPIES THE FIRST SEVEN FLOORS OF THE HISTORIC BEACON BUILDING ON THE CITY'S EAST SIDE.
"FOUNDED JUST SIX YEARS AGO, G.G.M. IS NOW ONE OF THE CITY'S FASTEST GROWING AND MOST PROFITABLE BANKS.
"ALL IN ALL, IT'S A LITTLE POWERHOUSE OF A PLACE.
"THREE-HUNDRED-AND-ELEVEN BILLION IN ASSETS. 12.2 BILLION IN EQUITY ALONE.
"IT'S GOT A GOOD REPUTATION AMONG ITS EMPLOYEES, TOO. OFFICIALLY, G.G.M. OPENS AT 8 AM.
"BUT MOST OF ITS PEOPLE ARE OUT FRONT BY 5 AM, WHEN THE BUILDING DOORS UNLOCK. TO GET AN EARLY START ON THE DAY.
"WHAT THEY FOUND IN THE LOBBY OF G.G.M. THIS MORNING, THOUGH..."

"...WAS OUT AND OUT ONE OF THE STRANGEST CRIME SCENES I'VE WORKED IN ALL MY YEARS IN GOTHAM.
"A KILLER WHALE. ORCINUS ORCA. A BLACK AND WHITE MONSTER OF A THING, LYING DEAD ON THE BANK FLOOR, ON A TUESDAY MORNING.
"NO CLUES AS TO WHO DID IT, HOW, OR WHY."

"A PLACE LIKE THAT MUST HAVE EYES ON THE FLOOR."

"PLENTY. BUT ALL THE CAMERAS ARE LOOPED TO A MAIN SERVER."

"AND WHAT, SOMEONE RAN A *BLINDFOLD?*"

"SEEMS THAT WAY. THE SERVER WENT DEAD FOR ALMOST AN HOUR LAST NIGHT, BETWEEN FOUR AND FIVE IN THE MORNING."

HUNGRY CITY

PART ONE OF THREE
SCOTT SNYDER: WRITER
JOCK: ARTIST & COVER
DAVID BARON: COLORS
SAL CIPRIANO: LETTERS

IT WENT COMPLETELY BLACK. POINT IS, DICK, WE HAVE *NOTHING*. WE'RE BLIND AS BATS.
SO CAMERA-SHY BAD GUYS IN GOTHAM...AT LEAST THEY'RE ORIGINAL.
LET'S FIRE UP THIS BAD BOY AND SEE WHAT WE SEE.
YOU KNOW, I'D BE REMISS IF I DIDN'T SAY THANKS TO ALL YOU WAYNES FOR OPENING YOUR DOORS TO THE G.C.P.D. YET AGAIN.
DON'T BE SILLY, COMMISSIONER. IT'S JUST NICE TO SEE THE DEPARTMENT FINALLY COMING AROUND.

SAYING THANK YOU, FROM ME. G.C.P.D. WANTED TO PROCESS THE WHALE AT COUNTY, BUT THE SAD TRUTH IS THE LAB THERE, IT COULDN'T HANDLE THE DAMN THING.
OUCH. LET'S KEEP THAT ONE FROM BRUCE. HE'S NOT A MAN USED TO THROWING PARTIES NO ONE SHOWS UP TO, IF YOU KNOW WHAT I MEAN.
OKAY, HERE WE GO. ACCORDING TO THE COMPUTER...
...THIS LOVELY LADY MOST LIKELY HAILS FROM THE BALMY AND BEAUTIFUL SIBERIAN SEA AND CLOCKS IN AT FORTY-THREE FEET LONG AND 4.2 TONS IN WEIGHT--WHICH IS ABNORMALLY LARGE FOR A FEMALE ORCA.
NO RECORD OF HER IN CAPTIVITY, BUT THE COLLAPSED DORSAL FIN SUGGESTS THAT SOMEONE WAS KEEPING HER CAGED.
SO SOMEONE WAS ILLEGALLY KEEPING HER AS A PET. POSSIBLY FEEDING HER GROWTH HORMONES. UNTIL WHAT, SHE GOT OFF THE LEASH?
ANYTHING ON THE BANK?

LIKE I SAID, THE LAST SIX YEARS G.G.M. HAS BEEN THE LITTLE BANK THAT COULD.
IT'S GROWN FASTER THAN ANY OTHER REGIONAL BANK, EVEN IN THIS CLIMATE. BUT IT'S ALL ABOUT SLOW AND STEADY INVESTMENT, NOTHING RISKY OR AGGRESSIVE.
NOTHING SUSPECT ON THEIR BOOKS.
EVEN SO, SOMEONE MUST BE TRYING TO SEND THE BANK A MESSAGE.
SO. QUESTION IS: A DEAD WHALE SHOWS UP IN THE LOBBY, WHO GETS THE MOST EGG ON HIS FACE?
HER.
WHAT?
HER FACE.
THE HEAD OF THE BANK IS A SHE. AND, TO BE HONEST, THAT'S ANOTHER REASON I WANTED TO COME HERE FIRST, DICK, BEFORE THE CASE BREAKS.
UM, COMMISSIONER? YOU'RE MAKING ME NERVOUS HERE...
HER NAME'S SONIA BRANCH.
DOESN'T RING A BELL.
SHE CHANGED IT TO BRANCH.
HER OLD NAME WAS ZUCCO, DICK. SONIA ZUCCO.

ZUCCO.
AS IN ANTHONY "FATS" ZUCCO.
THE MAN WHO KILLED YOUR PARENTS.
WOW...
-SIGH- WELL, AT LEAST WE KNOW WHERE TO START DIGGING.

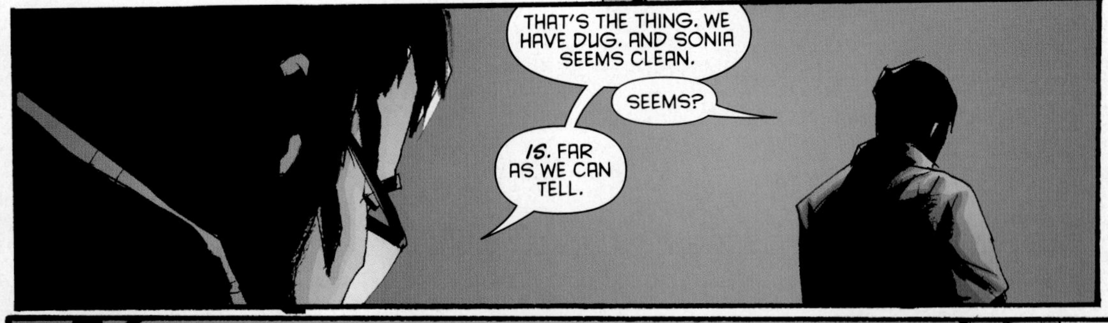
THAT'S THE THING. WE HAVE DUG. AND SONIA SEEMS CLEAN.
SEEMS?
IS. FAR AS WE CAN TELL.

SO TONY ZUCCO HAD A KID.
WHAT DO WE KNOW ABOUT THE MOM--
--OTHER THAN THAT SHE WAS BLIND, OBVIOUSLY?

THE MOM WAS A WAITRESS. RAISED SONIA HERSELF, WITH LITTLE TO NO CONTACT WITH TONY.
AS FOR SONIA, SHE WORKED HER OWN WAY THROUGH SCHOOL. HONORS. VALEDICTORIAN. GOLD STARS AND BUMPER STICKERS ALL AROUND.
AT TWENTY-FOUR, SHE STARTED G.G.M. NOW SHE'S A FORBES GIRL. LIKED BY HER EMPLOYEES, HER CO-WORKERS... SHE'S A HUGE SUCCESS STORY, DICK.
HUH. WELL, I GUESS IT'S NICE TO KNOW THAT MAYBE, ONCE IN A BLUE MOON, THE APPLE DOES FALL FAR FROM THE TREE IN GOTHAM.
ONCE IN A BLUE MOON.
ALL RIGHT, WE'RE ALMOST THROUGH, COMMISSIONER...
COMMISSIONER?
I'M SORRY, WHAT?
LISTEN, DON'T TAKE THIS THE WRONG WAY, BUT LATELY YOU'VE SEEMED A LITTLE... ***DISTRACTED.***
AND IF THERE'S ANYTHING YOU WANT TO TALK ABOUT...

...
IT'S MY SON. HE'S BACK IN GOTHAM.

JAMES?

HE SAYS...HE CLAIMS TO BE *DIFFERENT* NOW.

HE'S ON MEDICATION. SOMETHING CALLED DIAXAMYNE. IT'S NEW. I DID SOME CHECKING THOUGH, AND I SUPPOSE IT SEEMS ON THE LEVEL. I...I DON'T KNOW.
I WAS HOPING YOU MIGHT MEET WITH HIM.

ME?

I CAN'T...I CAN'T SEE THIS ONE CLEARLY, DICK. I'M TRYING TO, BUT...WHEN IT'S THIS CLOSE...

OF COURSE I'LL DO IT, COMMISSIONER. JUST SAY WHEN.
PROMISE ME SOMETHING, DICK.

PROMISE ME YOU'LL BE *HONEST* WITH ME. I NEED TO KNOW.
YOU SEE SOMEONE NEW, SOMEONE GOOD-- FINE. BUT YOU SEE SOMETHING ELSE--
RIIIPP

SSHRIIIIPPP
--SOMETHING SINISTER...

It's funny, back hen I was young, I ouldn't understand why Bruce never used the plane...
...why he always chose to drive the streets, moving on the ground through the alleys, when he could have just soared above it all.
But I get it now. Because even back then he understood that Gotham is a place you can never get above, a place you can never see clearly.
Every time you try to get some purchase, the city changes beneath you, surprising you in new, terrible ways.
So why try? That was Bruce's attitude back then. It's still his attitude now. You stay low, close to the fight. It's all about the fight now, today, in front of you.
I can't help it, though. I'm built differently. Because there's something about seeing Gotham from the sky that energizes me, gives me hope, if only for a moment...

...before I come back down to earth.
Sonia Branch, born Sonia Zucco, daughter of Tony Zucco, the man who **murdered my parents.**
It turns out the girl inside the whale was her personal assistant. A young woman by the name of Evelyn Marr.
By all accounts, Sonia and Evelyn were close. Girlhood friends.
The coroner's report suggests that Evelyn died inside the whale's stomach. Meaning she was **eaten alive.**
HELLO? IS SOMEONE THERE?
MS. BRANCH.

BATMAN?
WHY... WHY ARE YOU HERE?

TO HELP FIND EVELYN'S KILLER.
CAN I SPEAK WITH YOU FOR A MINUTE?

NO. NO YOU CAN'T. PLEASE...I ALREADY TOLD THE POLICE-- I DON'T KNOW ANYTHING.
SHE LEFT WORK ON FRIDAY AND THAT WAS THE LAST I SAW OF HER. I THOUGHT SHE WAS VISITING HER MOTHER... HER MOTHER'S IN THE HOSPITAL...

...OH GOD, EVELYN... -SNIFF-
I CAN'T...

SONIA. TALK TO ME.

PLEASE, YOU HAVE TO LEAVE. I HAVE OTHER PEOPLE CLOSE TO ME, PEOPLE THEY'LL COME AFTER--
WHO? WHO WILL COME AFTER--
I CAN'T... I CAN'T.
CLICK

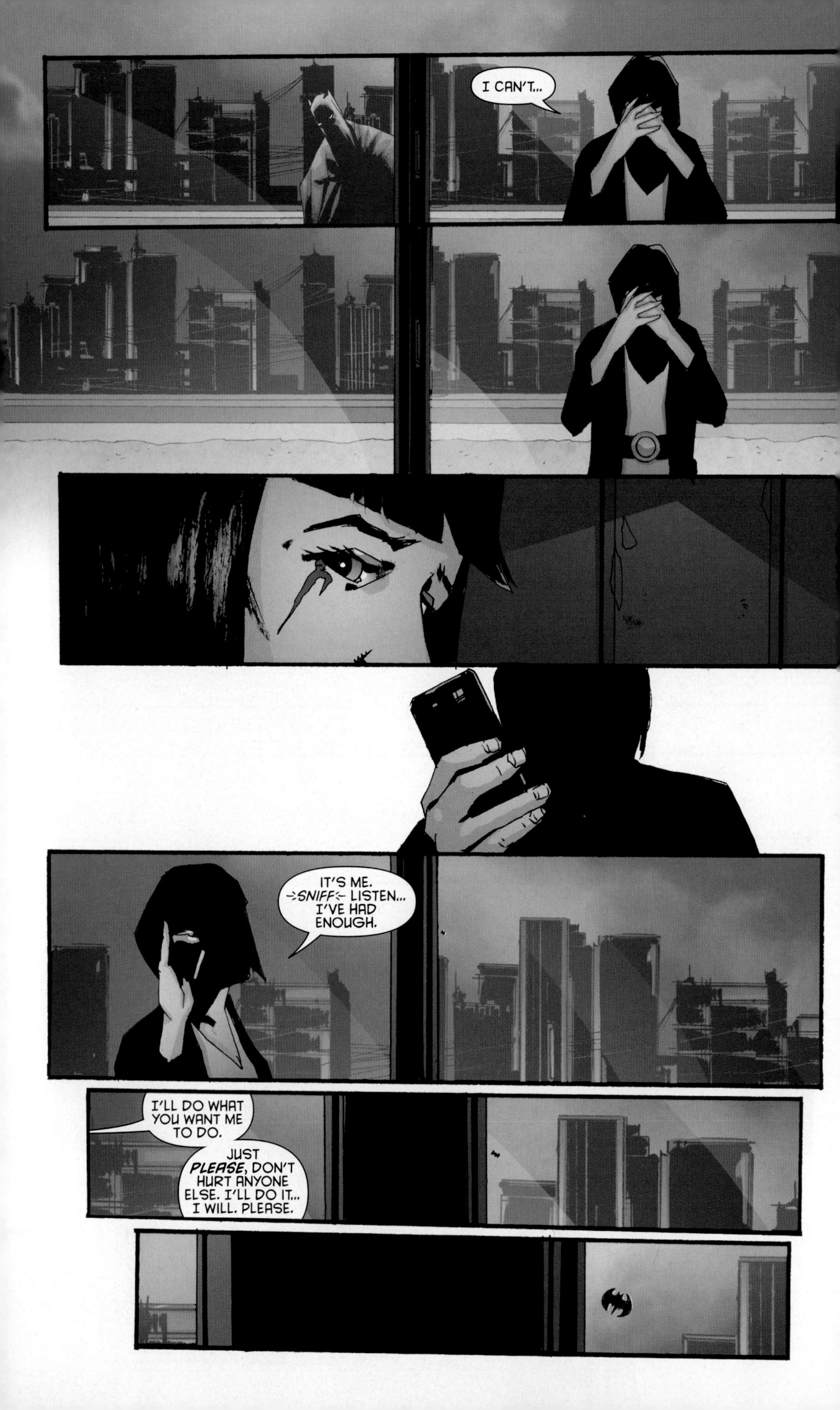
I CAN'T...
IT'S ME. -SNIFF- LISTEN... I'VE HAD ENOUGH.
I'LL DO WHAT YOU WANT ME TO DO.
JUST PLEASE, DON'T HURT ANYONE ELSE. I'LL DO IT... I WILL. PLEASE.

"JUST STOP THIS. STOP *HURTING* PEOPLE.
"PLEASE..."
Sonia Zucco--daughter of Tony Zucco, a known dirtbag and murderer. A lowlife thug for the Maroni Family.
NG...TRACING...
ING...TRACING...
ACING...TRACING...
020254065
ADDRESS ACQUIRED
0559000-0066-005
1700 00BW-GOTH
ADDRESS ACQUIRED
Sonia Branch--upstanding citizen. Gotham success story. Innocent victim...
...and there goes Gotham again... shifting right beneath my feet.

The number Sonia called belongs to a man named **Bixby Rhodes.**
He runs an extremely high-end car dealership here on the northern tip of Gotham.
He sells some of the most expensive cars in the world, customized to be even **more** expensive.
Cars with carbon fiber bodies, computerized windshields, diamond dust paint and 1,200 horsepower.
Word on the street is that in just the last year, he's become one of the city's premier gun smugglers.
He hides clients' weapons in custom-ordered luxury cars. The prize at the bottom of the cereal box.
He's a new guy, a new face on the street-- to me at least.

What's he after her f--
RATA TATATAT
RATA TATATAT
Stupid, Dick. Stupid...
When it comes to street crime, you've been spoiled for too long...
Old-school crooks. Guys with a code.
But this "Roadrunner"--Bixby Rhodes--he's not the Maronis, Dick. Not the Falcones. He's a new breed. Young and hungry and deadly seriou--

WHAT THE--
RUMMMBLE
OH NO.

CLANG
YOU KNOW, HOLLIS, GLANCING AT THE LOT...
...I THINK IT'S POSSIBLE WE OVER-ORDERED THIS MONTH. WHAT DO YOU THINK?
DEFINITELY, MR. RHODES.
ALL RIGHT THEN...

"...LET'S REDUCE OUR INVENTORY...
"...START THE CRUSHER."

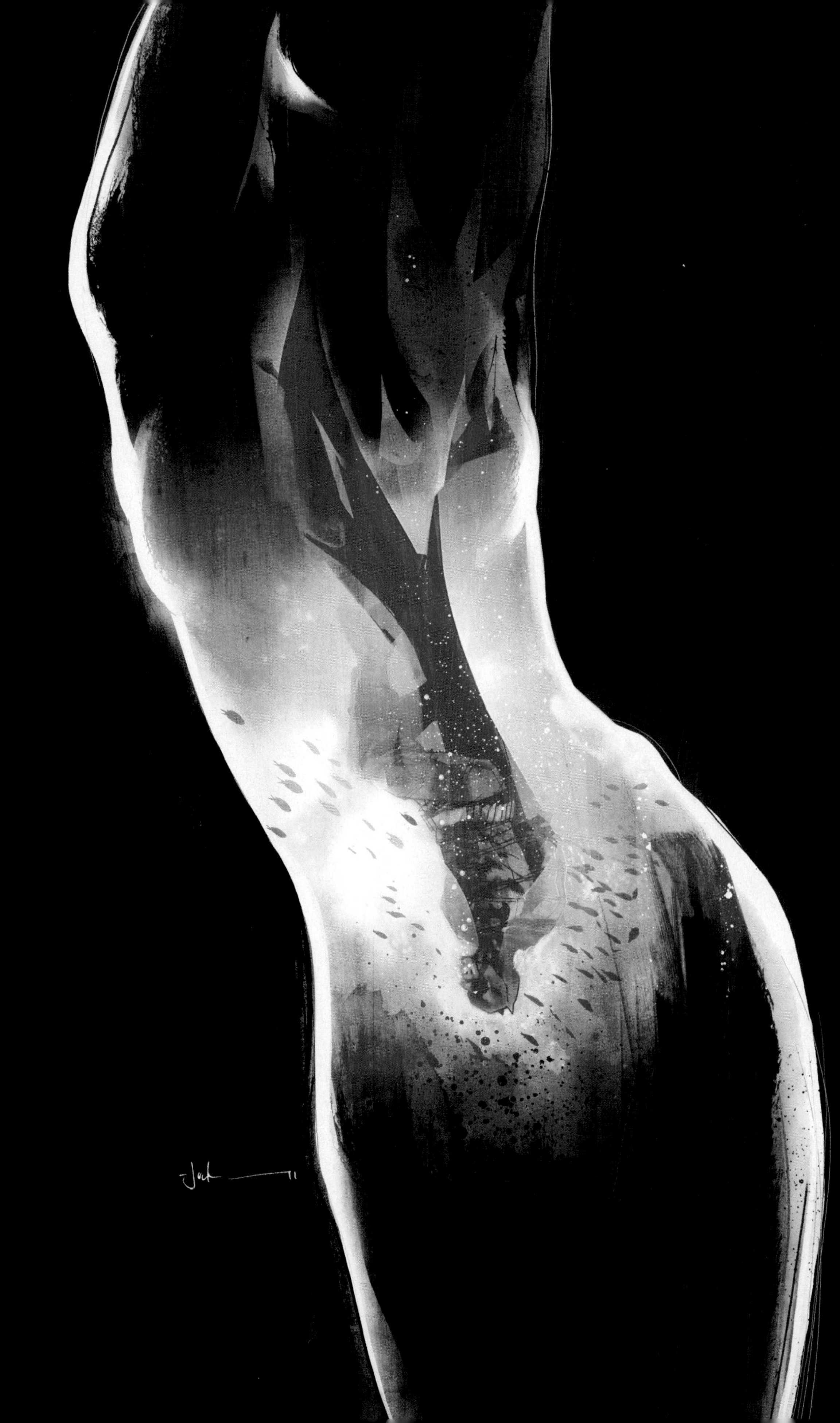

HUNGRY CITY

PART TWO OF THREE

There are moments it all feels ***hopeless****, this mission of ours.*

Moments when I can't help but wonder if it's all just one big ***dead end****.*

SCOTT SNYDER: WRITER JOCK: ARTIST & COVER
DAVID BARON: COLORS SAL CIPRIANO: LETTERS

ALL RIGHT, BATMAN, THINK... THE DOOR... IT HAS TO BE THE WEAKEST POINT.
I know the others must have moments like this, too--Bruce and Tim, even Damian--though we never really talk about it.
OF COURSE THERE'S NO BATTERY...
For me, the bad moments usually come in the morning, when I've just gotten home from patrol...
...the sun is just coming up, and I've spent the last ten hours dealing with some particularly disgusting example of humanity, the worst of the scum.
COME ON, DAMMIT! START!

VROOOM
Sometimes, when I'm too wound up to sleep, I'll watch nature shows. Shows on animals--meerkats, beluga whales--anything that doesn't have people in it...
As it happens, I caught a show on roadrunners the other night. It's funny, they're nothing like the cartoon. They're small and brown--aggressive predators.
One interesting thing about roadrunners is they're one of the few birds that're known to occasionally die from choking.
What happens is they try to swallow some small animal--a rat, a snake--before it's chewed up all the way.
The prey gets lodged in the roadrunner's throat... and the roadrunner, well, it actually ends up choking on its own meal.
Laid low by lunch.

The man who just tried to kill me--**Bixby Rhodes**--is a high-end weapons smuggler.
Moves guns in and out of Gotham in luxury cars. His associates call him the **"Roadrunner."**

Hey, if the shoe fits...

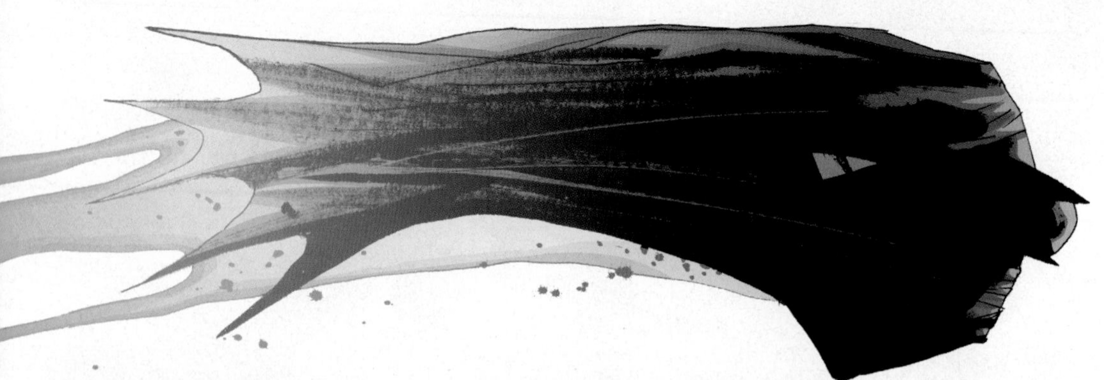

And now his lunch is **pissed.**
UNNNH!
CRAAASH

OVER HERE.
ANY SIGN OF HIM?
NOT YET, SIR, BUT HE HAS TO BE AROUND HERE SOME--

TIMOR? TIMOR, ARE YOU THERE?

ANSWER ME, DAMMIT! HAVE YOU...
...FOUND HIM...?
THIS IS THE PART WHERE YOU RUN.
ALL RIGHT, BATS. IF THAT'S THE WAY YOU WANT IT, THEN ALL I CAN SAY IS...
MEEP, MEEP, SUCKER.
Well, that's new...
Must be made from some kind of titanium alloy, the way they absorb the shock.

FORGET THIS...

HE'S AT THE TWENTY, THE TEN, AND HE--
ACCCK!
I SUPPOSE THIS IS THE PART WHERE I'D SAY, "B-DEEP, THAT'S ALL FOLKS"...
IF I HAD A SENSE OF HUMOR.
WHICH I DON'T.
SONIA BRANCH. WHY ARE YOU AFTER HER?

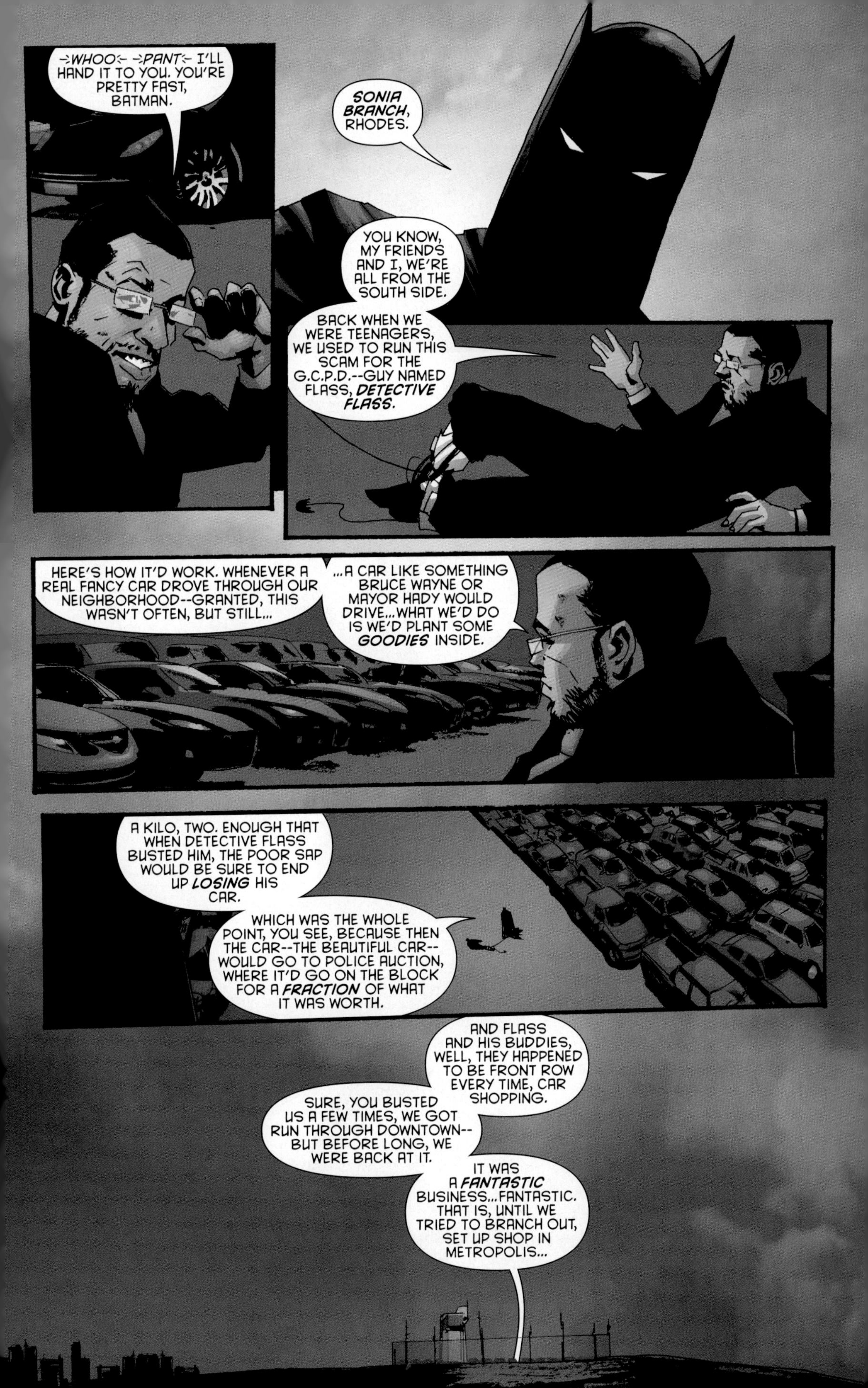
-WHOO- -PANT- I'LL HAND IT TO YOU. YOU'RE PRETTY FAST, BATMAN.
SONIA BRANCH, RHODES.
YOU KNOW, MY FRIENDS AND I, WE'RE ALL FROM THE SOUTH SIDE.
BACK WHEN WE WERE TEENAGERS, WE USED TO RUN THIS SCAM FOR THE G.C.P.D.--GUY NAMED FLASS, DETECTIVE FLASS.
HERE'S HOW IT'D WORK. WHENEVER A REAL FANCY CAR DROVE THROUGH OUR NEIGHBORHOOD--GRANTED, THIS WASN'T OFTEN, BUT STILL...
...A CAR LIKE SOMETHING BRUCE WAYNE OR MAYOR HADY WOULD DRIVE...WHAT WE'D DO IS WE'D PLANT SOME GOODIES INSIDE.
A KILO, TWO. ENOUGH THAT WHEN DETECTIVE FLASS BUSTED HIM, THE POOR SAP WOULD BE SURE TO END UP LOSING HIS CAR.
WHICH WAS THE WHOLE POINT, YOU SEE, BECAUSE THEN THE CAR--THE BEAUTIFUL CAR--WOULD GO TO POLICE AUCTION, WHERE IT'D GO ON THE BLOCK FOR A FRACTION OF WHAT IT WAS WORTH.
AND FLASS AND HIS BUDDIES, WELL, THEY HAPPENED TO BE FRONT ROW EVERY TIME, CAR SHOPPING.
SURE, YOU BUSTED US A FEW TIMES, WE GOT RUN THROUGH DOWNTOWN--BUT BEFORE LONG, WE WERE BACK AT IT.
IT WAS A FANTASTIC BUSINESS...FANTASTIC. THAT IS, UNTIL WE TRIED TO BRANCH OUT, SET UP SHOP IN METROPOLIS...

...I STILL REMEMBER THE MORNING IT HAPPENED...IT WAS A TUESDAY. SUNNY OUT.
I WAS JUST ROLLING UP IN MY WHEELCHAIR TO THIS GEM, A 1979 SKYHAWK, BLACK AS NIGHT WITH CHROME TRIM.

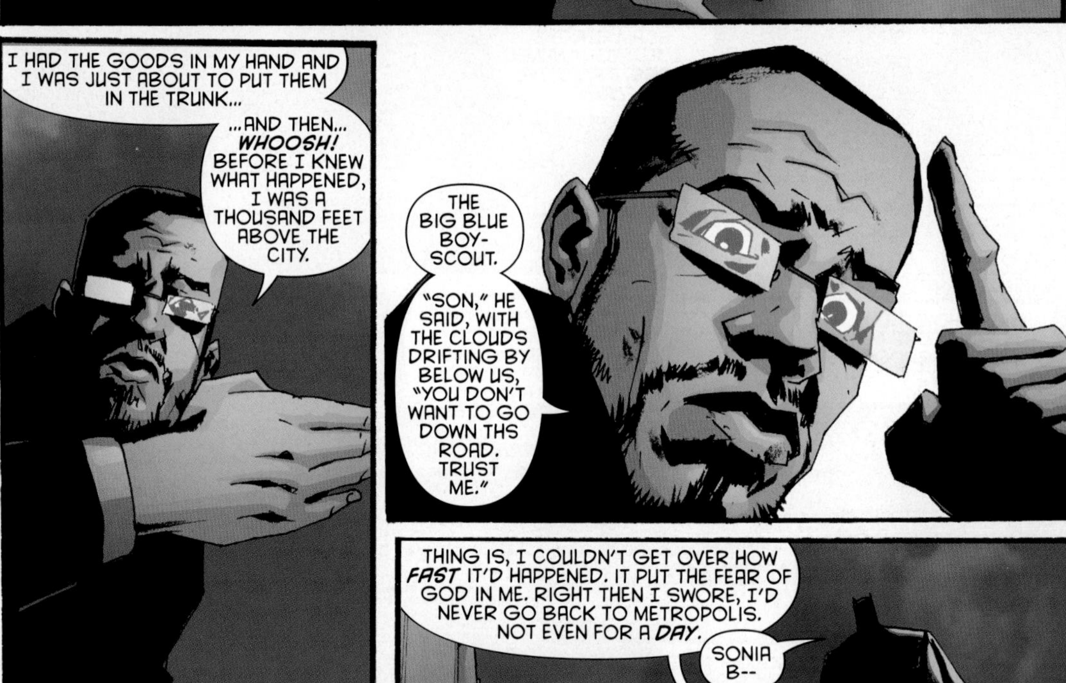
I HAD THE GOODS IN MY HAND AND I WAS JUST ABOUT TO PUT THEM IN THE TRUNK...
...AND THEN... **WHOOSH!** BEFORE I KNEW WHAT HAPPENED, I WAS A THOUSAND FEET ABOVE THE CITY.
THE BIG BLUE BOY-SCOUT.
"SON," HE SAID, WITH THE CLOUDS DRIFTING BY BELOW US, "YOU DON'T WANT TO GO DOWN THS ROAD. TRUST ME."

THING IS, I COULDN'T GET OVER HOW ***FAST*** IT'D HAPPENED. IT PUT THE FEAR OF GOD IN ME. RIGHT THEN I SWORE, I'D NEVER GO BACK TO METROPOLIS. NOT EVEN FOR A ***DAY***.
SONIA B--
SONIA BRANCH. I KNOW.

BUT SEE, THAT'S WHAT I'M TRYING TO ***TELL*** YOU. METROPOLIS IS A CITY WHERE ***GODS*** WALK THE STREETS.
BUT ***GOTHAM?*** IT'S A CITY OF ***MEN***. AND UNDER THAT MASK, YOU'RE JUST A ***MAN***. SAME AS ***ME***.
WHICH IS ALL ONE WAY OF SAYING, *HEH, HEH*...I AIN'T TELLING YOU--
CRUNCH

OH NO. WHAT A KLUTZ I AM. HERE, LET ME HELP YOU UP.

WHAT--YOU GOT NOTHING ON ME! *NOTHING!* WHERE ARE YOU TAKING ME?

OH, I THOUGHT I COULD SHOW YOU MY CAR AND SEE IF THERE'S ANYTHING YOU THINK I COULD DO TO MAKE IT A LITTLE *SWEETER*...

...YOU BEING SUCH AN *AFICIONADO* AND ALL...

"HE HAS YOU, YOU KNOW..."

...YOU WERE TRESPASSING, AND ANYTHING EVEN REMOTELY SOLID WAS DESTROYED IN THAT BEHEMOTH OF A CRUSHER.
WHICH IS TO SAY BIXBY RHODES WILL LIKELY BE BACK ON THE STREETS IN A FEW DAYS.
YEAH, BUT JUST RUINING HIS WEEK MAKES THE RAIN FEEL A LITTLE LESS WET, DOESN'T IT?
YES, IT DOES.
STILL, WHAT PUTS A DAMPER ON THINGS IS THE COMPLETE LACK OF CONNECTION BETWEEN OUR ROADRUNNER AND THE WHALE-ZILLA LYING ON THAT BANK FLOOR.
ALL OF WHICH HAS ME THINKING THAT SONIA BRANCH-- SONIA ZUCCO--IS HIDING SOMETHING, COMMISSIONER.
WHO KNOWS, MAYBE THE ROTTEN APPLE DOESN'T FALL SO FAR FROM THE TREE IN GOTHAM, AFTER ALL.
BATMAN, WE SPOKE AGAIN WITH MS. BRANCH.
AND?
AND, YOUR SUSPICIONS ARE SPOT ON--

--I *WAS* HIDING SOMETHING.
BUT I'M NOT HIDING ANYMORE.
SHE'S BEEN WAITING TO SPEAK WITH YOU. SHE SAID SHE NEEDED TO TALK TO YOU, ALONE.
YOU *CAN* SAY NO.
IT'S FINE.

I APOLOGIZE. I DIDN'T TELL YOU EVERYTHING THE OTHER NIGHT. BUT I WAS... SCARED.
SCARED OF WHO?
YOU.
YOU HAVE NOTHING TO BE SCARED OF FROM ME UNLESS YOU'RE--
A CRIMINAL? LIKE MY FATHER?
I'M ASHAMED OF ANTHONY ZUCCO, BATMAN. I SHOULDN'T HAVE TO BE. I BARELY KNEW HIM--MY MOTHER BARELY KNEW HIM...
...BUT THE FACT IS, I'VE SPENT MY WHOLE LIFE TRYING TO GET OUT FROM UNDER THAT NAME. TRYING TO BE MY OWN PERSON...
...BUT I SUPPOSE SOMETIMES OUR FATHERS' SHADOWS-- THEY'RE LARGER THAN WE'D LIKE.

BECAUSE NO MATTER WHAT I DO, SOME PEOPLE WILL *ALWAYS* SEE ME AS THE DAUGHTER OF TONY ZUCCO. THUG. MURDERER. COWARD.
AND MAYBE I WAS WRONG, BUT AT THAT MOMENT, I COULDN'T IMAGINE ANYONE MORE LIKELY TO SEE ME THAT WAY... THAN *YOU*.
YOU WEREN'T WRONG.
BUT I'M HERE NOW... AND I'M LISTENING.
EVER SINCE *GOTHAM MODERN* TOOK OFF, I'VE GOTTEN ACCOUNT REQUESTS FROM SOME OF GOTHAM'S NASTIER ELEMENTS--CRIMINALS WHO WANT US TO HELP THEM INVEST THEIR MONEY.
CLEAN IT, YOU MEAN.

EXACTLY. AS YOU CAN IMAGINE, WITH MY FAMILY HISTORY, THEY CAME EXPECTING AN OPEN DOOR. IT'S BEEN THAT WAY SINCE WE STARTED OUT.
IT USED TO BE THE FAMILIES-- THE FALCONES, THE MARONIS.
BUT TO THEM, I SAID NO, AND THEY TIPPED THEIR HATS AND WALKED AWAY.
BUT THESE NEW GUYS... THEY DON'T TAKE "NO" FOR AN ANSWER. I THOUGHT I COULD HANDLE THEM, BE TOUGH, BUT I WAS *WRONG*.
WHO ARE THEY?
THE TWO WORST, THE ONES WHO HAVE BEEN THREATENING US FOR WEEKS, ARE BIXBY RHODES--THE ROADRUNNER-- WHOM YOU MET ALREADY...
...AND A SMUGGLER, A GUY WHO CALLS HIMSELF ***TIGER SHARK***. HE'S A PIRATE. COLD-BLOODED KILLER.
I'VE NEVER EVEN MET HIM. HE SENT A MAN INTO THE BANK TO INQUIRE ABOUT AN ACCOUNT.
I TURNED HIM DOWN. HE WARNED ME. I TURNED HIM DOWN AGAIN. AND THE NEXT THING I KNOW, EVELYN IS MISSING... AND...
WHERE IS HE?
I DON'T KNOW. THEY SAY HE LIVES ON SOME KIND OF ***BOAT*** OFF SHORE, OUTSIDE THE JURISDICTION OF THE COAST GUARD.
I WISH I KNEW MORE. I DO. I'M SORRY...
NO, ***I'M*** SORRY, MS. BRANCH. BUT I'LL MAKE IT UP TO YOU...

"...STARTING RIGHT NOW."

LET ME GET THIS STRAIGHT...

...YOU SAID "ROTTEN APPLE" AND SHE WAS **RIGHT BEHIND** YOU?

I APOLOGIZED... SORT OF.
HANG ON, I'M TAPPING INTO G.C.P.D. ROOF SECURITY CAM...
HA! YOUR FACE. THAT IS A BAT-MEME IF I'VE EVER SEEN ONE...
AND WOW. MS. BRANCH IS BEGUILINGLY ATTRACTIVE. WHY IS THAT? WHY ARE THERE NO AVERAGE MOBSTERS' DAUGHTERS?
SHE'S NOT EXACTLY YOUR STANDARD MOBSTER'S DAUGHTER. SHE'S MADE A PRETTY HERCULEAN EFFORT TO DISTANCE HERSELF FROM HER FATHER.
OH, COME ON. TELL ME YOU'RE NOT INTO HER. SHE'S THE DAUGHTER OF TONY "FATS" ZUCCO.
I'M NOT INTO HER.
AND THAT SOUNDED CONVINCING.
RED ROBIN? OH, NO. YOU'RE BREAKING UP.
BATMAN. YOU'RE ON 5G. I CAN' BREAK UP.
RED ROBIN?
IT'S SCIENTIFICALLY IMPOSSIBLE FOR OUR CONNECTION TO--
CLICK

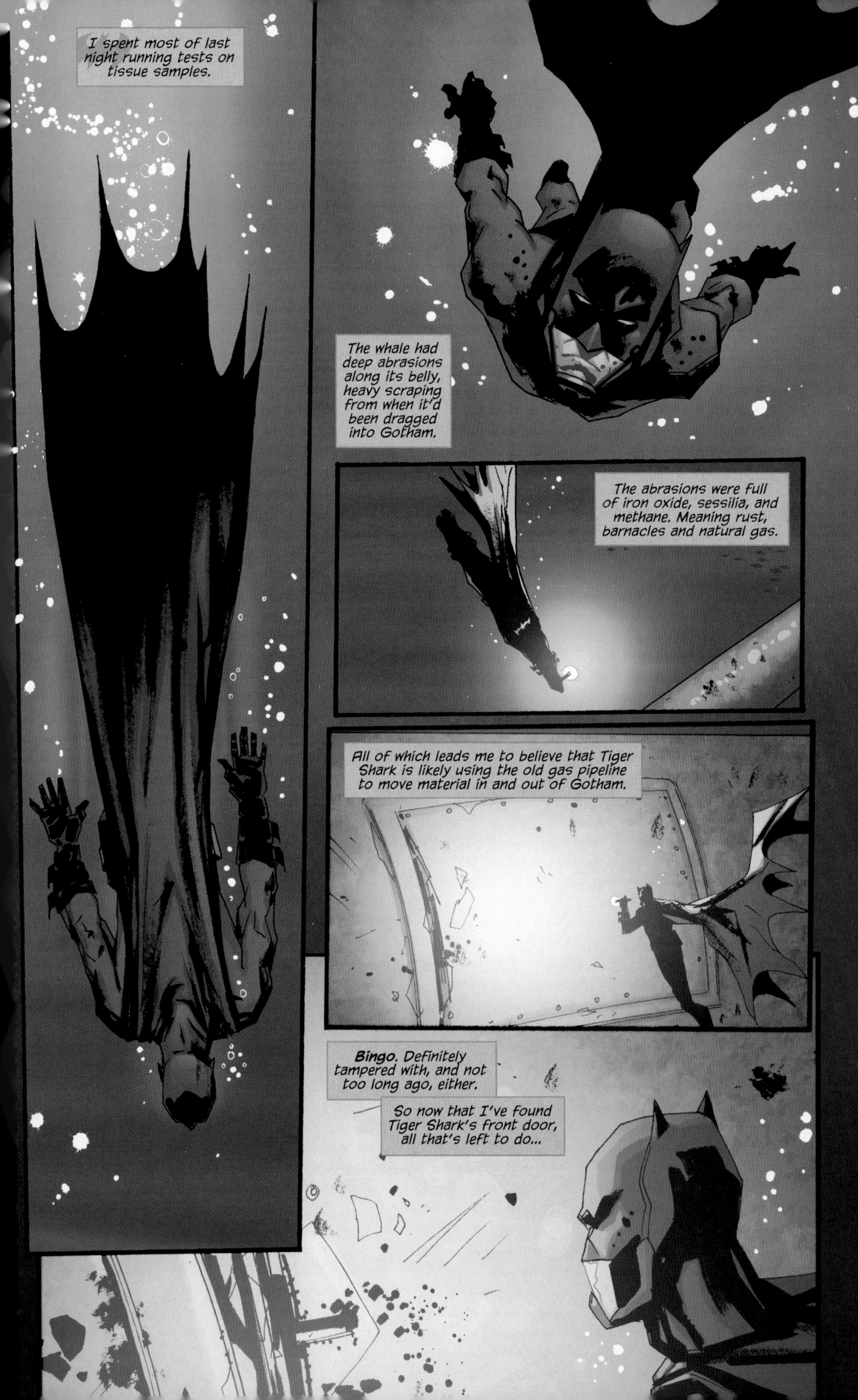
I spent most of last night running tests on tissue samples.
The whale had deep abrasions along its belly, heavy scraping from when it'd been dragged into Gotham.
The abrasions were full of iron oxide, sessilia, and methane. Meaning rust, barnacles and natural gas.
All of which leads me to believe that Tiger Shark is likely using the old gas pipeline to move material in and out of Gotham.
Bingo. Definitely tampered with, and not too long ago, either.
So now that I've found Tiger Shark's front door, all that's left to do...

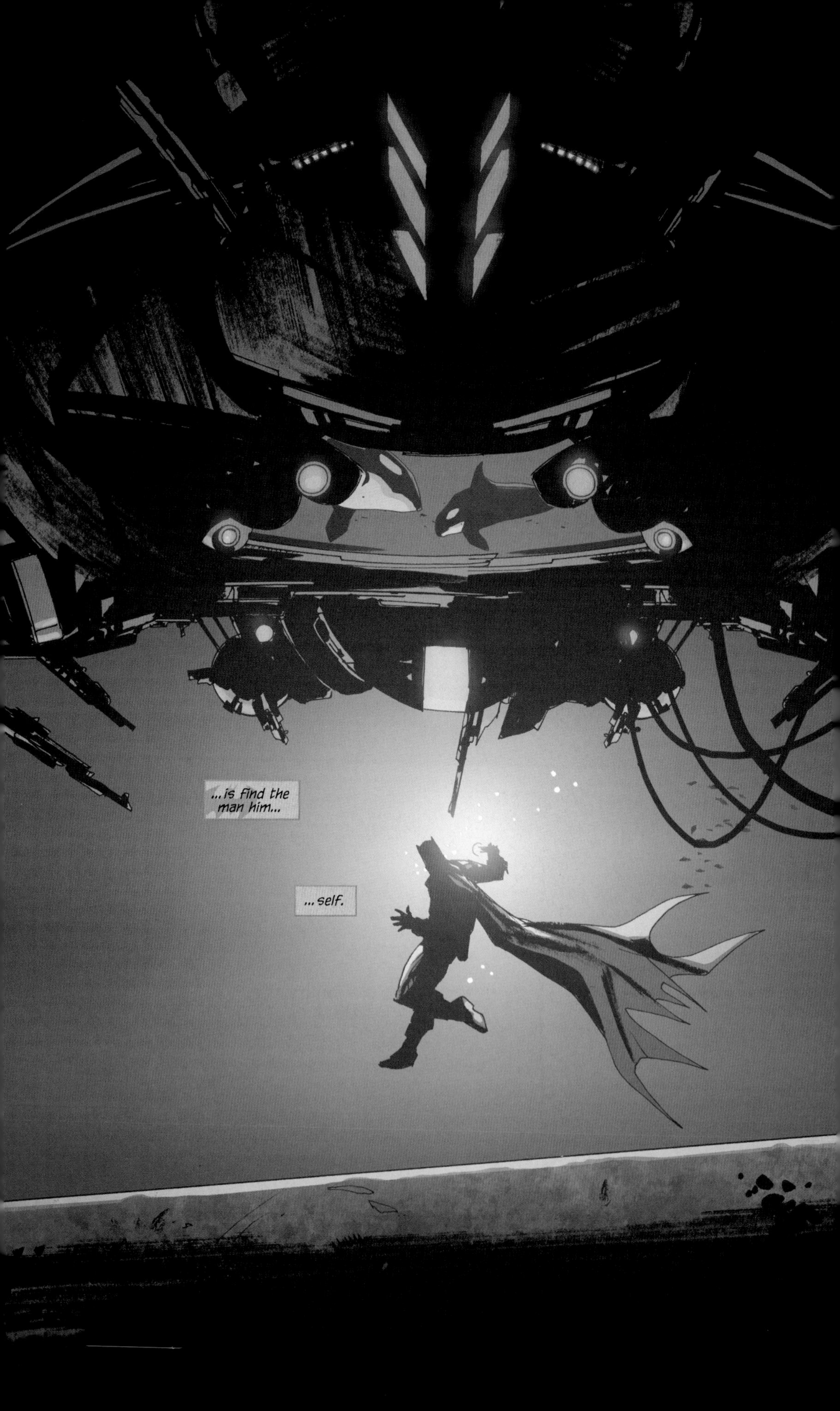
...is find the man him...
...self.

-Jock

There are two kinds of performers in a circus. The **"seasonals"** and the **"lifers."** The seasonals come and go. The lifers are all in, **always.**

My parents were lifers. Lifers stuck with other lifers. We sat together in the dining tent, watched each other's kids...

...one man I remember watching me a number of times was a high-diver named Francis Roy.

His stage name was the **"Dive Bomber,"** and in his act, he would climb to the top of an eighty-foot tower, and then dive off...

...plunging into a tank of water less than **three feet deep.**

It was mesmerizing to watch. I remember one time, when he was babysitting me, I asked him what the trick was, how he dived into such a shallow tank without breaking his neck?

And he said to me, "Dickie boy, it's all about **judgment**. Early judgment.
"Meaning, you have to judge the situation right away, **from the diving board.** Before you jump. Not from the air, but from the board."

I think it's fair to say that on this one, I **missed** the diving board altogether.
The man in the mask calls himself **Tiger Shark.**
He's a pirate, a high-end trafficker of material in and out of Gotham City.
He's wanted for the murder of a young woman named **Evelyn Marr**, assistant to banker **Sonia Branch.**
Evelyn was found in the belly of a whale just like the one below me. **Eaten alive.**
My assumption was that Tiger Shark killed Evelyn to intimidate Sonia into laundering money for him.
But I'm starting to think that maybe, he killed her just for **fun.**

TIGER SHARK WILL ASK YOU ONE LAST TIME, BATMAN.
WHAT WERE YOU DOING SO FAR FROM SHORE, IN HIS WATERS?
PRACTICING MY BACKSTROKE. NOW ASK TIGER SHARK WHY HE KILLED EVELYN MARR?
HEH HEH...
TIGER SHARK SAYS, TODAY, MANY PEOPLE THINK THAT THE ACT OF FORCING SOMEONE TO "WALK THE PLANK" IS A MYTH. BUT IN TRUTH, IT WAS A VERY REAL TRADITION DURING THE GOLDEN AGE OF PIRACY IN THE 17TH CENTURY.
IN FACT, THERE WERE SOME CAPTAINS WHO MADE SUCH FREQUENT USE OF THE ACT THAT SHARKS WOULD FOLLOW THEIR SHIPS FOR THOUSANDS OF MILES, WAITING FOR THE MOMENT SOME POOR FELLOW WOULD BE FORCED OFF INTO THE BLUE.
THE MORE VICIOUS PIRATE CAPTAINS WOULD EVEN TEASE THE SHARKS ON OCCASION, BY FORCING ONE OF THEIR OWN CREW OFF THE BOAT IN ADVANCE OF THE REAL VICTIM, JUST TO WHET THE SHARKS' APPETITE...
...SOME OLD OR SICKLY MEMBER OF--
NO!

AAAIIEE!
DO YOU SEE TIGER SHARK'S TIE? IT'S MELANISTIC JAGUAR. DO YOU SEE HIS SHOES? KING COBRA. HIS SUIT? MADE FROM THE BACKS OF ANGEL SHARKS.
HE WEARS CLOTHING MADE FROM ONLY THE RAREST, MOST "ENDANGERED," OF NATURE'S CREATURES.
WHY, YOU ASK HIM, BATMAN? BECAUSE WHILE YOU CALL TIGER SHARK A PIRATE, A SMUGGLER, HE IS, IN TRUTH, PART OF A PROUD LINEAGE--
-- THE SEA PEOPLE OF ANTIQUITY...

...THERE IS A RECORD OF US AS EARLY AS THE TEMPLES OF RAMESES II, IN THE SECOND MILLENNIUM B.C..
COME HERE, SAYS TIGER SHARK, BATMAN. COME HERE AND SEE.
WE HAVE BEEN RESPONSIBLE FOR THE CULTIVATION--AND THE DESTRUCTION-- OF SOME OF HISTORY'S GRANDEST CIVILIZATIONS. HITTITE, MYCENAEAN, MITANNI...

"...WE ARE BRINGERS OF LUXURY, BATMAN, OF CULTURE AND LANGUAGE, OF FOLKLORE AND *MYTH*. WE SAIL WITH THE TIDES, FOR WE ARE THE CHILDREN OF THE SEA."
LOOK, LOOK UPON HIM!

FOR HE IS A KING! A KING OF THE S--
CRACK
YES, AND THAT, TOO.
A KING WHO MURDERS INNOCENT YOUNG WOMEN TO BULLY AND INTIMIDATE PEOPLE.
SHWAP
SPLOOSH

HUUPPRRSUNCS UCTVVUTT
TRANSLATE... TRANSLATE...
"HYPERSONICS ACTIVATE."

CRASSH
AAAGH!
LOOK AT YOU GO, BATMAN! YOU ARE A RARE CREATURE.
KRAK

IF ONLY I'D HAD MORE TIME, I WOULD HAVE TAKEN PIECES OF YOUR WONDERFUL SKIN TO LINE MY SHOES.

ALAS, THERE IS NO TIME TODAY.

FOR I AM AFRAID THE SEA CALLS ME AWAY.

JUST AS IT CALLS TO YOU, BATMAN. FOR THE TRUTH IS THAT IN THE END, WE ALL GO BACK TO THE SEA. THE TIDES WILL RECLAIM US.

SO TO PUT IT TRUTHFULLY, I AM SIMPLY SHEPHERDING YOU HOME A LITTLE EARLY.

He booby-trapped the yacht.
Of course he did. I want to say I saw it coming. I want to say something witty, but all I can think is...
...well played, sir.
BOOM BOOM
Because with a blast hole that big, the ship will take less than a minute to flood.
And worse, the tide of water will be pushing into the vessel, so it'll be near impossible for a man caught inside to fight his way out through the current.

But even if he was able to escape, he'd be nearly 1,000 feet beneath the surface of the ocean by my best estimate.
And at that depth, the pressure would be nearly **unbearable** for him.
Besides, even if his suit were equipped to withstand the pressure, he'd still have to be able to hold his breath long enough to reach the surface.
A feat that'd take even a great swimmer roughly... seven minutes? Which would be near impossible for anyone.

Well... except, maybe, someone who's downright overcautious (or who's been **trained** to be overcautious) when it comes to seafaring missions...
...and so makes sure to boost his oxygen levels by ingesting significant amounts of pure O_2 in advance.
If the guy in question--if he was that **crazy**, maybe--just maybe--he'd squeak by?
BATMAN! BATMAN, IS THAT YOU? WE'VE GOT A SIGNAL FROM YOU AGAIN.
AHOY.

PHEW. AND YOU'RE ALL RIGHT?
REPORTS OF MY DEATH ⇒KOFF KOFF⇐... I'M FINE. JUST **HURRY**...

"...I HAVE AN IMPORTANT APPOINTMENT TO KEEP."

JAMES?

JAMES GORDON? IS THAT YOU?
HELLO, DICK.

WOW. YOU'RE...IT'S YOU. I MEAN IT'S WEIRD, ISN'T IT? THE WAY YOUR MENTAL IMAGE OF SOMEONE DOESN'T AGE?
IT'S CALLED HELMUT-GREEBLE PHENOMENON, ACTUALLY. OR THE "GLACIER EFFECT." AS IN YOUR BRAIN PRESERVES YOUR MEMORY OF A PAST ACQUAINTANCE THE SAME WAY A GLACIER PRESERVES DEAD REMAINS.
THANK YOU FOR MEETING WITH ME, DICK.
OF COURSE. LESLIE TOLD ME HOW WELL YOU'RE DOING AT THE CLINIC, HELPING HER OUT, AND I WANTED TO EXPRESS MY THANKS IN PERSON.
IT'S OKAY, DICK. I KNOW YOU'RE HERE ON BEHALF OF MY FATHER. AND I'M GRATEFUL YOU ARE.
TRUTHFULLY, IF MY FATHER WASN'T SKEPTICAL OR SUSPICIOUS OF ME AT THIS POINT, I'D PROBABLY QUESTION HIS POLICE SKILLS.
THAT WAS A JOKE.
AH. SORRY.
BUT YES, IF WE'RE BEING UPFRONT, YOUR FATHER DID ASK ME TO REPORT BACK AFTER WE MET.
WHICH I UNDERSTAND MUST BE DAUNTING, SEEING AS WE HAVEN'T SEEN EACH OTHER IN WHAT, TWELVE YEARS? SINCE THAT DAY WE HAD THE PICNIC.

RIGHT! THE PICNIC IN THE PARK. WITH BARBARA AND THAT OTHER BOY.
BEN WOLFF.
BEN WOLFF! AND HE TOOK YOUR GLASSES AND BURIED THEM...AND BABS PUSHED HIM IN THE POND FOR IT. I REMEMBER NOW.
GOD, WHAT A TOOL THAT GUY WAS. *HA.* WHAT WAS YOUR SISTER *THINKING?*
WE WERE ALL JUST KIDS. I ACTUALLY BUMPED INTO BEN THE OTHER DAY.
REALLY?
I DID. HE'S A PHARMACEUTICAL REPRESENTATIVE NOW.
HE LIVES OVER ON THE EAST SIDE. HE WAS NICE AS COULD BE.
FUNNY, THE WAY SOME PEOPLE TAKE A WHILE TO GROW INTO THE PEOPLE THEY'RE GOING TO BE.
I KNOW! WHILE OTHER PEOPLE NEVER...
...CHANGE...
DICK?
JAMES, I'M SO SORRY. I HAVE TO GO.
ARE YOU SURE?
I AM. AGAIN, I'M SORRY...

"...THERE'S SOMETHING I OVERLOOKED."
IT WAS YOU, WASN'T IT?
BATMAN?
YOU KILLED THE VIDEO FOOTAGE OF TIGER SHARK'S MEN PLACING THE WHALE IN YOUR LOBBY.
THE WHALE WITH EVELYN'S BODY INSIDE.
I DON'T KNOW WHAT YOU--
NO ONE ELSE COULD'VE ACCESSED THE BUILDING'S SECURITY SYSTEM.
YOU BLACKED IT OUT, SO I WOULDN'T KNOW WHO TO GO AFTER. THEN YOU DELIBERATELY SENT ME AFTER RHODES FIRST, EVEN THOUGH HE HAD NOTHING TO DO WITH EVELYN'S DEATH.
YOU USED ME TO TAKE THEM DOWN IN THE ORDER YOU WANTED.

I HARDLY KNOW HOW TO RESPOND TO THAT, BATMAN.
AFTER ALL, ROADRUNNER AND TIGER SHARK, THEY'RE NOT THE CRIMINALS OF OLD. I'D HAVE TO BE PRETTY *CUNNING* TO OUTDO THEM.
DON'T SELL YOURSELF SHORT.
ALL RIGHT, SUPPOSING-- AND JUST SUPPOSING--I DID USE YOU TO TAKE THEM BOTH DOWN, WOULD THAT BE *SO WRONG?*
THEY WERE HARASSING ME TO LAUNDER MONEY FOR THEM. THEY *KILLED MY FRIEND.*

YOU'D BE GUILTY OF OBSTRUCTING THE LAW.

HA! THE *LAW?* YOU'RE GOING TO STAND THERE, TRESPASSING ON MY PROPERTY, IN A MASK AND CAPE, AND TALK TO ME ABOUT THE *LAW?*
MAN, I NEED A DRINK.
YOU TAMPERED WITH EVIDENCE AND REDIRECTED THE INVESTIGATION. IT'S ARGUABLE THAT HER KILLER, TIGER SHARK, ESCAPED BECAUSE YOU WASTED TIME BY SENDING ME AFTER RHODES FIRST.

TRUE. THEN AGAIN, IT'S ARGUABLE THAT HER KILLER, TIGER SHARK, ESCAPED BECAUSE *YOU* FAILED TO CATCH HIM--ISN'T IT, BATMAN?

YOU SAY TOMATO, I SAY YOU'RE CULPABLE.

WE'LL HAVE TO AGREE TO DISAGREE, WON'T WE THEN?
GOOD NIGHT, BATMAN.
GOODNIGHT, MS. ZUCCO.
IT'S MS. BRANCH.
THAT'S WHAT I SAID.
You have to judge the situation early, clearly...

...judge it from the diving board, high above, before you're falling...before you're in danger.
That's what Francis Roy used to say. I can still picture his act, too. Picture him up there, standing at the top of his tower, so high above the crowd, above us all...
...looking down at the water, assessing the drop.
It's funny to think that no one knew that that's where the real feat happened--in that quiet moment before, not the jump, but the perfect judgment.

It never got old, his act. As a boy, I watched Roy do it dozens, even hundreds of times.
I was even watching the day he got it wrong.
WOLFF
The day he misjudged...
WOLFF
...and hit the water just a degree or two off point.
He broke his neck, dying instantly.

HELLO, BEN. GUESS WHO I JUST MET WITH? YOUR OLD FRIEND DICK GRAYSON.

YEP. WE WERE JUST TALKING ABOUT YOU! ISN'T THAT *FUNNY?*

LEEEEAASEEEE. LEASSSSE...

NOW, WHERE WERE WE?

HUNGRY CITY

PART THREE OF THREE

SCOTT SNYDER: WRITER JOCK: ARTIST & COVER

DAVID BARON: COLORS SAL CIPRIANO: LETTERS

SKELETON KEY

SCOTT SNYDER

FRANCESCO FRANCAVILLA

Come here. No, closer... I want to TELL you a story...
it's A story about love.
Love, LovE, love!
There once was a boy, a nicE boy...and he loved a girl.
TIGHTEN HIS MASK, WILL YOU? THANKS.
And the Boy and the girl loved each other soooo much...
...and at first, Every-thing seemed WONDERFUL!

Ooohhh... But then something BAD happened... Something so terrible.
THAT'S AS TIGHT AS HIS MASK GOES?
AFRAID SO.
This terrible thing, though, it didn't happen right away...not right away. No... see, at first...

"...everything
eemed just fine."
I KNOW, BUT IT'S THE TRUTH. HE'S BEEN A HUGE HELP, JIM.
E RE-FILED THE V.A. TRANSFER RECORDS.
HE SET UP A NEW SITE FOR US ONLINE.
HE HAULS LAUNDRY. HE MOPS. HE DUSTS. HECK, HE EVEN VOLUNTEERED TO START MAKING OUR NUTRITION RUNS NEXT WEEK.
JAMES GO
SURE, HEH HE'S A LITTLE NTENSE, BUT FOR HE MOST PART, VERYONE REALLY LIKES HIM. HE'S POPULAR.
JAMES JR., PROM KING.
AND WHAT DOES BARBARA THINK OF ALL THIS?
BABS? DOESN'T BUY IT FOR A SECOND.
WELL THAT'S A SHAME. BUT HE'S DOING WELL. HE'S MAKING FRIENDS. EVEN REKINDLING OLD CONNECTIONS.
JUST THE OTHER DAY HE WAS TALKING ABOUT LOOKING UP SOME OLD FRIEND OF HIS, A CHILDHOOD BUDDY?
ALL I'M SAYING IS IT'S OKAY TO LET YOURSELF BE A LITTLE HAPPY, JIM.
I'M WORKING ON IT.
WORKING ON WHAT?

JAMES. WE WERE--
I WAS JUST TELLING YOUR OLD WORKHORSE OF A FATHER HERE TO TRY AND SLOW DOWN A BIT. ENJOY HIMSELF IN HIS OLD AGE.
HE NEEDS TO TAKE UP A HOBBY. YOGA. PAINTING.
IT HELPS ME, HAVING HOBBIES.
I'VE GOT TO GET BACK. BUT JAMES, SWING BY LATER TO MAKE SURE WE TRACK ALL THE EXTRA HOURS YOU SPENT MAKING RUNS YESTERDAY.
I WILL, MS. THOMPKINS.
JAMES...IF YOU CALL ME MS. THOMPKINS ONE MORE TIME, YOU'RE FIRED. LESLIE. LESLIE.
LESLIE.

SHOULD O, TOO. AVE TO T BACK.
OF COURSE.
OKAY THEN. SEE YOU SOON.
DAD!
THANKS FOR COMING BY.

RUN DIAGNOSTIC AGAIN. BUT ROUTE THROUGH THE MINOR LOOP THIS TIME. THEN--
...CONTINUING?
PAUSE FOR NOW.
WE NEED TO TALK ABOUT YOUR BROTHER, BARBARA.

'VE SAID
MY PIECE
ALREADY.
WELL, *I* HAVEN'T.
{SIGH} LET ME GUESS. YOU VISITED HIM AT LESLIE'S. AND HE SEEMS LIKE A REGULAR BOY SCOUT. SHE HAS HIM HELPING OUT ALL OVER THE PLACE, BUSY, BUSY BEE.
THAT'S RIGHT.
SEE, THAT'S JUST WHAT I'M TALKING AB--
WHICH IS WHY IT TOOK ME SO LONG TO GET A MOMENT ALONE AT HIS DESK.
AND PILFER ONE OF THESE THINGS...

I TOOK ONE FROM THE PILL BOTTLE IN HIS DRAWER. IT'S CALLED ***DIAXAMYNE.*** IT'S STILL IN TRIALS.
BUT IT'S SHOWN PROMISING RESULTS IN THE TREATMENT OF PSYCHOPATHY.
ACCORDING TO PUBLISHED STUDIES, IT STIMULATES PEPTIDE PRODUCTION IN THE PART OF THE BRAIN THAT CONTROLS HUMAN EMOTION.
IT HELPS PEOPLE WITH SEVERE ANTISOCIAL NEUROLOGICAL FUNCTION EXPERIENCE ***EMPATHY.***
IT MAKES PSYCHOS FEEL ALL WARM AND FUZZY INSIDE. I ***GET*** IT, DAD. WHY ARE YOU GIVING IT TO ME? AS SOME KIND OF ***PROOF*** OF JAMES' RECOVERY?
NO, BARBARA.
I'M GIVING IT TO YOU BECAUSE I WANT YOU TO ***TEST*** IT.
TEST IT?

WITH THE PILL IN TRIALS, THE COMPONENTS ARE GUARDED INFORMATION. BREAKING INTO THE PARENT COMPANY'S DATABASE WOULD BE ILLEGAL.
BUT YOU CAN BREAK THE PILL DOWN INTO ITS COMPONENTS HERE, SO WE KNOW WHAT'S IN IT.
THEN WE JUST HAVE TO GET LESLIE TO GIVE US JAMES' RESULTS FROM ONE OF THE STANDARD SCREENS SHE RUNS ON ALL HER VOLUNTEERS.
AND WE CAN SEE IF HE'S ACTUALLY ON THE LEVEL.
AND IF HE'S NOT? IF HE'S YING ABOUT TAKING THE PILLS?
IF HE'S NOT, AT LEAST WE KNOW HE'S UP TO SOMETHING. JUST LIKE YOU THINK HE IS.
BUT IF THE TEST COMES BACK AND HE IS TAKING THE MEDICINE?
CAN I ASK YOU SOMETHING, DAD? WHY COME TO ME? WHY NOT USE FORENSICS? OR THAT CRIME LAB THE WAYNES OPENED UP.
THE TECH THERE IS TOP GRADE. THIS'LL TAKE ME AT LEAST AN HOUR TO PROCESS. DICK GRAYSON COULD--
I ALREADY ASKED DICK HIS OPINION ON JAMES. AND FOR THE RECORD, BETWEEN US, I WAS WRONG TO DO IT.

THIS IS BETWEEN US...BETWEEN FAMILY. BLOOD.
OKAY. LET'S DO IT.
BETWE BLOO UNDE STAND
"But I was telling you a STORYYYY..."

About a girl and a boy IN love.
NURSE WILL NOTE PATIENT'S BLOOD PRESSURE IS ONE-TWELVE OVER SIXTY-FOUR. NORMAL.
And the boy, he was a doctor, like you. And the girl, see, she was a teacher.
DEEP BREATH... NURSE WILL NOTE THE PATIENT'S LUNGS SOUND AVERAGE.
she taught fourth grade. That is, until SHE GOT sick...
...she got sick with a bad, bad cold.
THAT'S ENOUGH, JOKER.
A cold calllled multiple sssssssclerosis.
SOMEBODY STOP HIM TALKING, PLEASE?
And the boy, the DOCTOR, he's so sad now, because the girlll, she screams and screeeeams at night. she's IN soo much pain (hee hee hee heeeeee!)
SHUT UP!

He can't even TOUCH HER anymore because she's in so much PAIINNN. He takes her to the Gotham aviary on good days...to look at the birds.
HOW DO YOU KNOW ABOUT MY WIFE?
DOC, DON'T LET HIM GET TO YOU.
To look at the BIRDSSS, her in her chair, shaking in pain, hee-hee!
HOW DO YOU KNOW THAT? TELL ME HOW, YOU BASTARD!
FUNNY, I LOVE the aviary myself, doc. You know what ROOOM is my favorite?
The "Birds of Melanesia." So pretty! THERE'S ONE bird I love in there from NEW GUINea called a Little Shrikethrush. A plain little thing. "Average," you could say. "Normal."
YOU HAVE PEOPLE WATCHING US?! YOU BASTARD!
HOW COULD YOU...
...KNOW?

STEP AWAY FROM HIM, DOC!
DOC?
HEE HEE HEE!
THERE'S SOMETHING ON JOKER'S SKIN! SOME KIND OF POISON! HE MUST'VE TAKEN SOMETHING...HE'S SECRETING SOME KIND OF TOXIN!
AAIIEEEE!
But (hee-hee) the shrikethrush is actually toxic to the touch. The buggies it EATS make its feathers POISONOUS...
See, that's the THING about normal and average. It seems harmless, but it's NOTTT...

MY GOD...
WHAT IS IT?
HE...HE *INVERTED* IT. THE FORMULA.
INVERTED WHAT? WHAT DO YOU MEAN?
THE PILL YOU TOOK, THE MEDICINE IN IT--IT'S NOT DESIGNED TO STIMULATE ACTIVITY IN THE AMYGDALA. IT'S DESIGNED TO *BLUNT* IT.
SEE THIS? IT'S A MIS-FOLDED PROTEIN. A "PRION." IT *ATTACKS* SPECIFIC PARTS OF THE BRAIN.
WHAT PARTS?
WHATEVER PARTS IT'S PROGRAMMED TO. BUT KNOWING JAMES...
KNOWING JAMES, IT'S DESIGNED TO ATTACK THE SAME PART OF THE BRAIN DIAXAMYNE IS SUPPOSED TO HELP.
HE'S HOPING TO TURN PEOPLE INTO...
PSYCHOPATHS LIKE HIM.

HOW, HOUGH? HAT'S HIS PLAN?
WELL, HE CAN'T JUST TOSS THE STUFF INTO THE RESERVOIR. IT'LL GET CLEANED OUT AT THE TREATMENT PLANT.
BESIDES-- AND HERE'S THE GOOD NEWS--LUCKILY, THE POTENCY IN THE FORMULA HE'S MADE, IT'S RELATIVELY LOW... 'M NOT SURE THAT IT'D HAVE A TREMENDOUS EFFECT ON THE ***ADULT BRAIN*** ANYWAY.
MAYBE ON CHILDREN, BUT STILL...

OH NO...

WHAT IS IT?

LESLIE. SHE SAID HE'D VOLUNTEERED TO DO ***NUTRITION RUNS*** FOR THEM.
WHAT ARE NUTRITION RUNS?

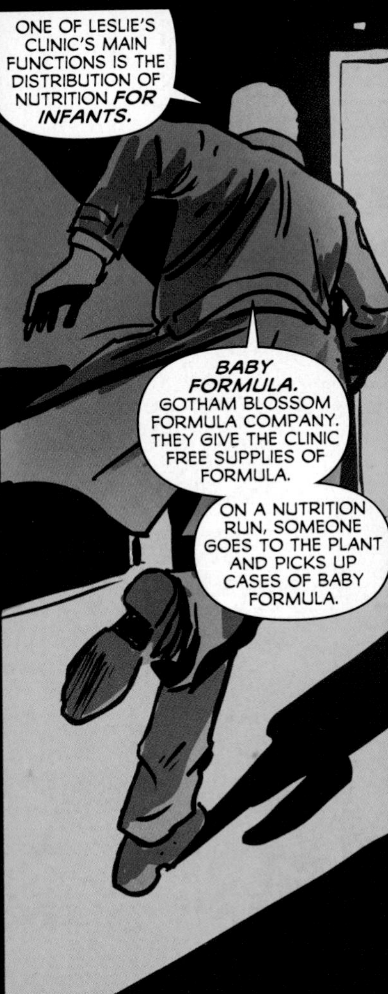
ONE OF LESLIE'S CLINIC'S MAIN FUNCTIONS IS THE DISTRIBUTION OF NUTRITION ***FOR INFANTS.***
BABY FORMULA. GOTHAM BLOSSOM FORMULA COMPANY. THEY GIVE THE CLINIC FREE SUPPLIES OF FORMULA.
ON A NUTRITION RUN, SOMEONE GOES TO THE PLANT AND PICKS UP CASES OF BABY FORMULA.

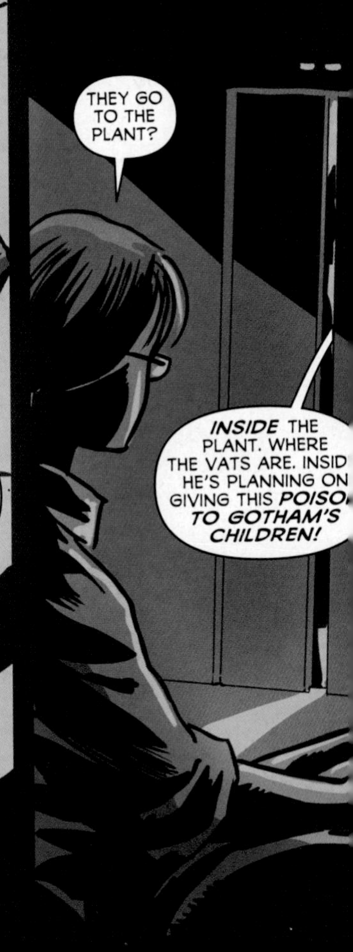
THEY GO TO THE PLANT?
INSIDE THE PLANT. WHERE THE VATS ARE. INSID HE'S PLANNING ON GIVING THIS ***POISO TO GOTHAM'S CHILDREN!***

"STOP HIM! HE'S ESCAPING!"
"NO...STAY AWAY!"
VROOOM
"Shhh! I was telling a story, and I'm almost AT THE END!"
"AAAAGG!"
"It's a story ABOUT LOVE!"
"LOVE!"
"LOVE!"
SKREE
"LOVE!"

JAMES!
JAMES, COME OUT AND...
DAMN.

JIM?
JIM, SOMETHING'S COME UP.

HAHAHAHAHAHAHAHAHAHA
"It's the Joker.
"He's out.
"Jim?"
JIM, EVERYTHING OKAY?
NO, HARVEY...

NOTHING'S OKAY.
SNYDER S. 11
FRAN CAVIL LAF. 11
HAPPY DAY
SKELETON KEY
SCOTT SNYDER
FRANCESCO FRANCAVILLA
LETTERS JARED K. FLETCHER

Gotham. It's a city of glass and concrete, of steel and brick.
And yet for me, like most people here, there's a city beneath the one I can see and smell and feel below my tires right now.
A city of memory. With a geography that only I know.
Where the biggest buildings, the most important landmarks, are the ones where something happened to me. Some tragic bulletin. A first kiss.
And after all these years, my city, the one beneath the glass and steel, is full of plenty of bright streets and dark alleys.
But the darkest spots on the map, the looming black towers, were almost all created by one man--the Joker.
In many ways, he's Gotham's darkest ar most brilliant archite

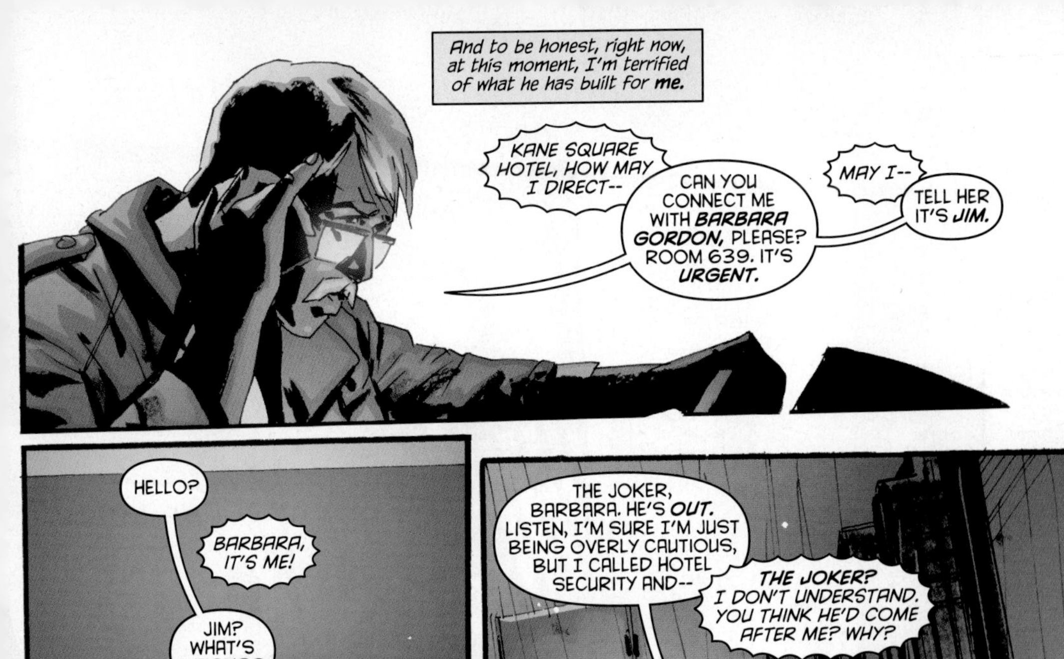

And to be honest, right now, at this moment, I'm terrified of what he has built for **me.**
KANE SQUARE HOTEL, HOW MAY I DIRECT--
CAN YOU CONNECT ME WITH **BARBARA GORDON,** PLEASE? ROOM 639. IT'S **URGENT.**
MAY I--
TELL HER IT'S **JIM.**

HELLO?
BARBARA, IT'S ME!
JIM? WHAT'S WRONG?
THE JOKER, BARBARA. HE'S **OUT.** LISTEN, I'M SURE I'M JUST BEING OVERLY CAUTIOUS, BUT I CALLED HOTEL SECURITY AND--
THE JOKER? I DON'T UNDERSTAND. YOU THINK HE'D COME AFTER ME? WHY?
I DON'T KNOW. BECAUSE THAT'S WHO HE **IS,** BARB. HE ALWAYS COMES AFTER US, OUR FAMILY. ANYONE I CARE ABOUT. LIKE I SAID, THESE ARE JUST PRECAUTIONS, BUT **PLEASE,** JUST STAY IN THE ROOM 'TIL I ARRIVE.
BUT HOW COULD HE KNOW WHERE--
BECAUSE HE ALWAYS KNOWS, DAMMIT!
PLEASE, BARB, I'M LIKELY WRONG, BUT YOU NEED TO PROTECT YOURSELF JUST IN CASE! NOW WHEN HOTEL SECURITY--

KNOCK KNOCK
WAIT, JIM? THEY'RE AT THE DOOR NOW. HOLD ON.
GOOD. JUST GO WITH THEM, BARBARA...
I'M PULLING UP DOWN-STAIRS NOW.
YES? WHO IS--
CRASH

BARBARA? BARBARA, WHAT'S HAPPENING?!
NO! DON'T! PL--
BARBARA! NO! ARE YOU THERE?
-HEE- -HEE- HEEEEEEEE-
LISTEN TO ME, YOU PIECE OF FILTH. YOU HURT HER AND I'LL--
CLICK
HELLO? HELLO?! DAMN!
BARBARA!
BARBARA, ARE YOU HERE?

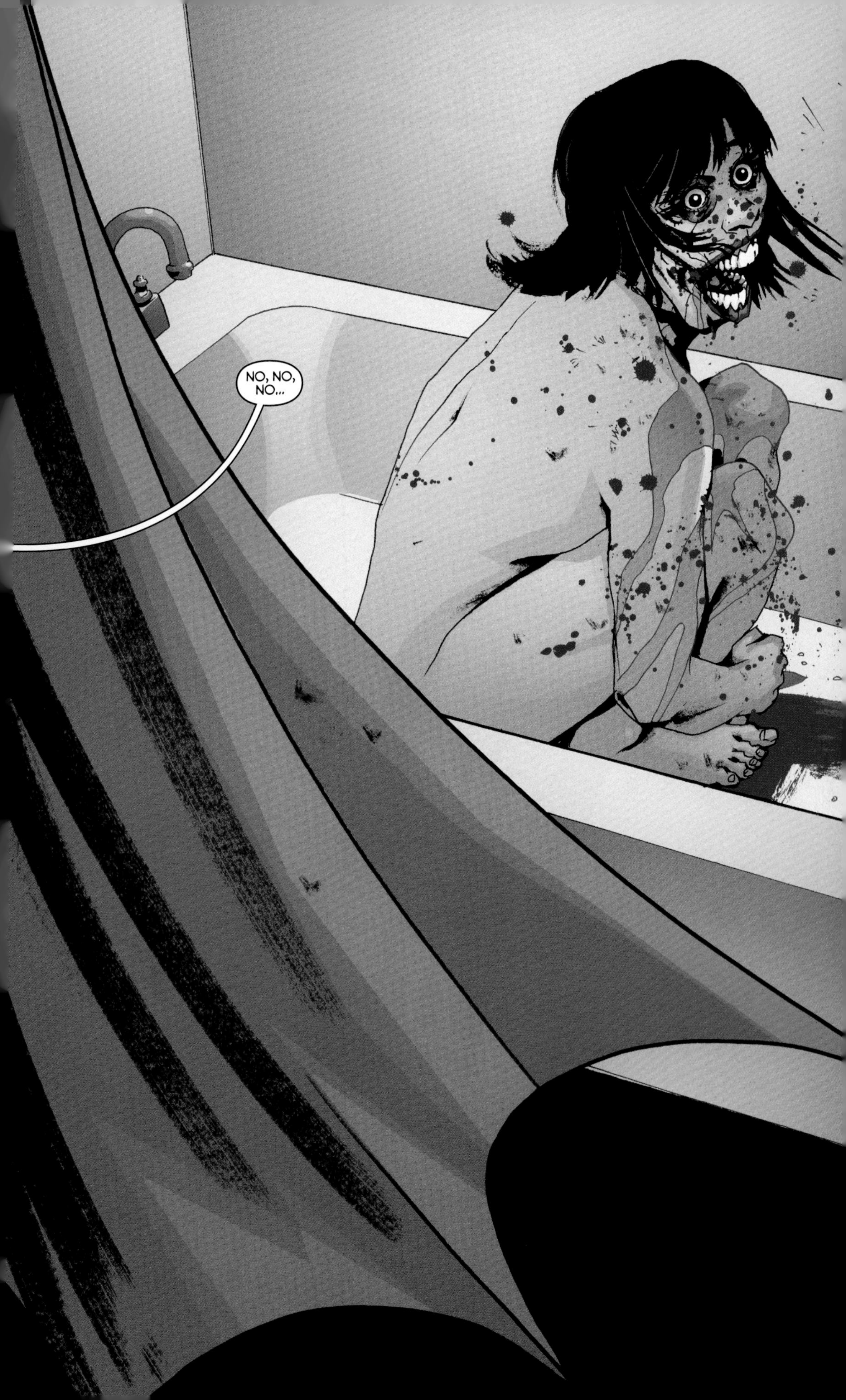
NO, NO, NO...

HER SIGNS ARE PROMISING, COMMISSIONER. SHE'S STILL CRITICAL, BUT WE WERE ABLE TO HALT THE PROGRESSION OF THE JOKER TOXIN.
NOW IT'S JUST A MATTER OF CAREFUL EXTRACTION. REMOVING THE TOXIN WHILE MAKING SURE SHE DOESN'T GO INTO SHOCK.
STILL, IF I'D GOTTEN THERE A MINUTE EARLIER--
IF YOU'D GOTTEN THERE A MINUTE LATER, DAD, SHE'D LIKELY BE DEAD, IS WHAT DICK'S SAYING.

I'LL CHECK IN ON THE HOUR.
BARBARA, YOU KNOW HE MIGHT BE AFTER *YOU,* TOO.
I'M NOT HIDING FROM HIM, DAD. HE WANTS ME? LET HIM COME KNOCK ON MY DOOR.
THIS TIME I'LL BE *WAITING.*

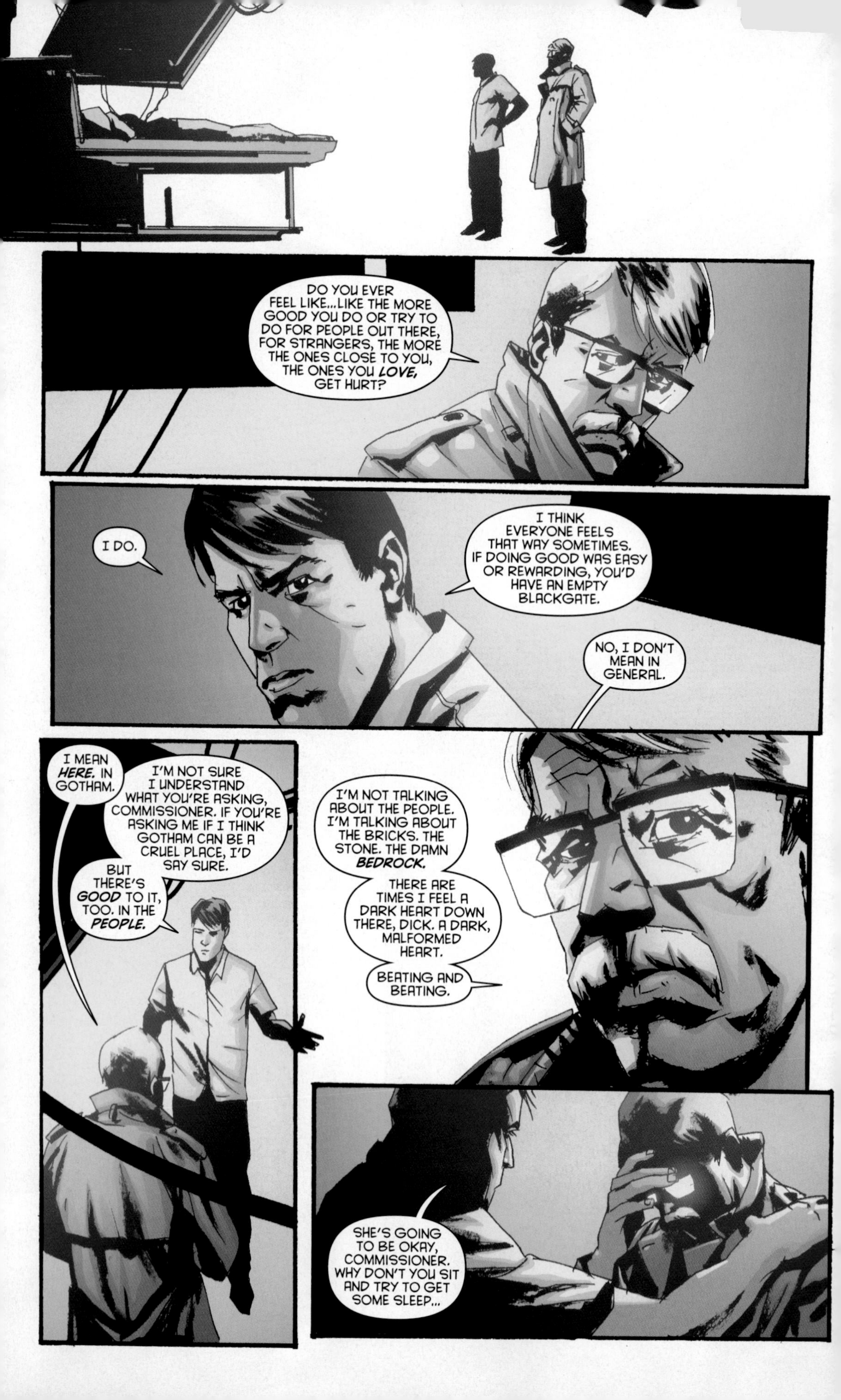
DO YOU EVER FEEL LIKE...LIKE THE MORE GOOD YOU DO OR TRY TO DO FOR PEOPLE OUT THERE, FOR STRANGERS, THE MORE THE ONES CLOSE TO YOU, THE ONES YOU *LOVE,* GET HURT?
I DO.
I THINK EVERYONE FEELS THAT WAY SOMETIMES. IF DOING GOOD WAS EASY OR REWARDING, YOU'D HAVE AN EMPTY BLACKGATE.
NO, I DON'T MEAN IN GENERAL.
I MEAN *HERE.* IN GOTHAM.
I'M NOT SURE I UNDERSTAND WHAT YOU'RE ASKING, COMMISSIONER. IF YOU'RE ASKING ME IF I THINK GOTHAM CAN BE A CRUEL PLACE, I'D SAY SURE.
BUT THERE'S *GOOD* TO IT, TOO. IN THE *PEOPLE.*
I'M NOT TALKING ABOUT THE PEOPLE. I'M TALKING ABOUT THE BRICKS. THE STONE. THE DAMN *BEDROCK.*
THERE ARE TIMES I FEEL A DARK HEART DOWN THERE, DICK. A DARK, MALFORMED HEART.
BEATING AND BEATING.
SHE'S GOING TO BE OKAY, COMMISSIONER. WHY DON'T YOU SIT AND TRY TO GET SOME SLEEP...

"...I'M GOING TO GO SEE WHAT I CAN FIND OUT."
WE KNOW THE TOXIN WAS SLIPPED INTO HIS FOOD.
AND THAT IT WAS A HIGHLY TOXIC, SATURATED FORMULA. BUT HOW, WHO, AND WHEN? WE'VE GOT NOTHING, BATS.
ALL WE KNOW IS THAT OMETIME IN THE AST TWO DAYS, HE TOXIN WAS ONTRABANDED TO JOKER.
AND BEING IMMUNE, HE WAS ABLE TO INGEST IT AND SECRETE ENOUGH THROUGH HIS OWN PORES TO MAKE HIM DEADLY TO THE TOUCH.

-SIGH- WE'RE GOING TO HAVE TO PUT THAT BASTARD IN A *BUBBLE,* AREN'T WE? A REAL BUBBLE. IT'S GETTING--
HOLD ON, DETECTIVE BULLOCK.
YES?

WE RAN DIAGNOSTICS ON THE TOXIN AND FOUND SOMETHING STRANGE.
JOKER HAS USED MORE THAN *FIFTY* DIFFERENT VERSIONS OF THE TOXIN--THAT WE *KNOW* OF.

THE ONE HE USED ON HIMSELF AND ON BARBARA SR. IS ACTUALLY ONE OF THE ***OLDEST*** *FORMS.*
THE TOXICITY, THOUGH. HE NEEDED TO TAKE SOMETHING SO POTENT THAT IT WOULD MAKE HIS OWN SWEAT DEADLY TO THE TOUCH.

THAT'S THE THING. THIS FORMULA IS ACTUALLY *LESS* DEADLY THAN MORE RECENT VERSIONS OF THE TOXIN.
IT WAS MIXED WITH A REFINED ALCOHOL TO FACILITATE EXCRETION THROUGH THE PORES.
AND BARBARA SR.?

RECOVERING, LUCKILY.

"THE COMMISSIONER IS DOWN THERE WITH HER NOW..."
"AND THE VISUAL ON JOKER?"

ABS IS BACK T THE NEEDLE, VORKING ON C FEED FROM THE HOTEL.
HE SHOULD AVE SOME- HING SOON.
"I'M PATCHING IN HE FORMULA FOR HE JOKER TOXIN OW. TELL ME WHEN YOU'RE ABLE TO ISOLATE IT."
I'VE GOT HIS SCENT.
GOOD. LET'S KEEP THE LINE OPEN. OVER.
HEY, WHERE'RE YOU GOING? THE SERVER FOOTAGE SHOWS HIM HEADED TOWARD THE SQUARE.
BAIT AND SWITCH. IT WAS THE DOCTOR PLAYING JOKER.
OUR JOKER WENT THIS WAY...
"NOT IN THE EMPLOYEE STAIR- WELL. NOT IN THE FREIGHT... WHERE ARE YOU...?"

...AH. THERE YOU ARE.
BUT WHY SO SHY ALL OF A SUDDEN?
FACIAL RECOGNITION.
ENHANCEMENT REQUIRED.
ENHANCE AWAY.
SMILE FOR THE CAMERA, YOU BASTARD.
BABS? YOU THERE?
TIM? HOW'S BARBARA?
SHE'S NOT CONSCIOUS YET, BUT I WANTED YOU TO KNOW SHE'S STABLE.
THANK GOD. AND BATMAN?

HANG ON...
SECURING... SECURING... LINE SECURE.
I'M HERE, RED ROBIN. THE OXIN TRAIL LEADS TO THE ***SOUTH BOWERY UNNELS.*** ACCORDING TO POTENCY LEVELS, I'M RIGHT BEHIND HIM.
I HAVE YOU. THAT SYSTEM THOUGH ⇒ZZZT⇐ ON THE MAP IT DEAD-ENDS AT THE FOUNDATION OF THE ⇒ZZZT⇐ WATER STREET TRINITY CHURCH...
YEAH, WELL, WE ALL KNOW JOKER LIVES BY HIS ***OWN*** MAPS.
BUT THEN AGAIN...
...SO DOES ***BATMAN.***

THE CRYPT BENEATH THE CHURCH. IF HE'S IN THERE, THE WALLS ARE -ZZZZTT- SOLID MARBLE. EVEN THIS LINE WON'T -ZZZZTT-
BATMAN? -ZZSSZZTTT-
YOU CAN'T HIDE FROM ME, JOKER.
NO! OF COURSE NOT!
EVERYONE KNOWS BATS CAN SEE IN THE DARK!
CLIK
SO I SAY... LET THERE BE LIGHT!

AAAGH!
DEACTIVATE NIGHT VISION!
You're not MY BAT. My Bat has wings of fleshHHH...skin between the fingERSSSS.
You smell like feathers, little bird.
No, you're not a bat at all, are you? No, no no...

...But I SUPPOSE YOU'LL HAVE TO DOOOO!
I came down here to rest... to sleep and dream, and then to be born again, wet and new, when my bat returns!
But you're keeping me up! Keeping us all up!
me and my friends! heee-heeeeeeee. Eeee-heeeEEE!

Do you even know what Gotham means, little bird? Do you?!
It means a safe place for goats!
And do you know what preys on goats?
Bats...
...The bat MAKES THE GOAT sick. But every bat does this in its own way. And you, YOU'RE NOT MY BAT!
So you can't hurt me! ONLY he can hurt me. Only MY sick, sick BAT CAN!
MAYBE SO...

...BUT I'M ABOUT TO GET AN "A" FOR EFFORT.
NO MORE. NO MORE HURTING THE GORDONS.
The Gordons...oh, litttTle bird. Heee.. heeee...I didn't do anything to the old bitch. My Batman would know...know my work.
I misss him. Tell him to come home. Pleasse? Pretty pleeease. I don't want to Goooo to bed yet. I want to playyy. Tell him. Tellhimforme.
TELL HIM!
THE GORDONS!
The gordonsgordons gordons...DON'T YOU SEE, YOU IDIOT? It wasn't me! Wasn't me...

"...wasn't me, wasssn't me, wasn't me..."
BARBARA, THANK GOD. TAKE IT EASY, BARB.
JIM! JIM, HE WAS SO *CRAZY*.
"wasn't me, wasn't me, wasn't meee..."
wasn't meeeeeeee...
IT WAS HIM, JIM!
IT WAS *HIM!*

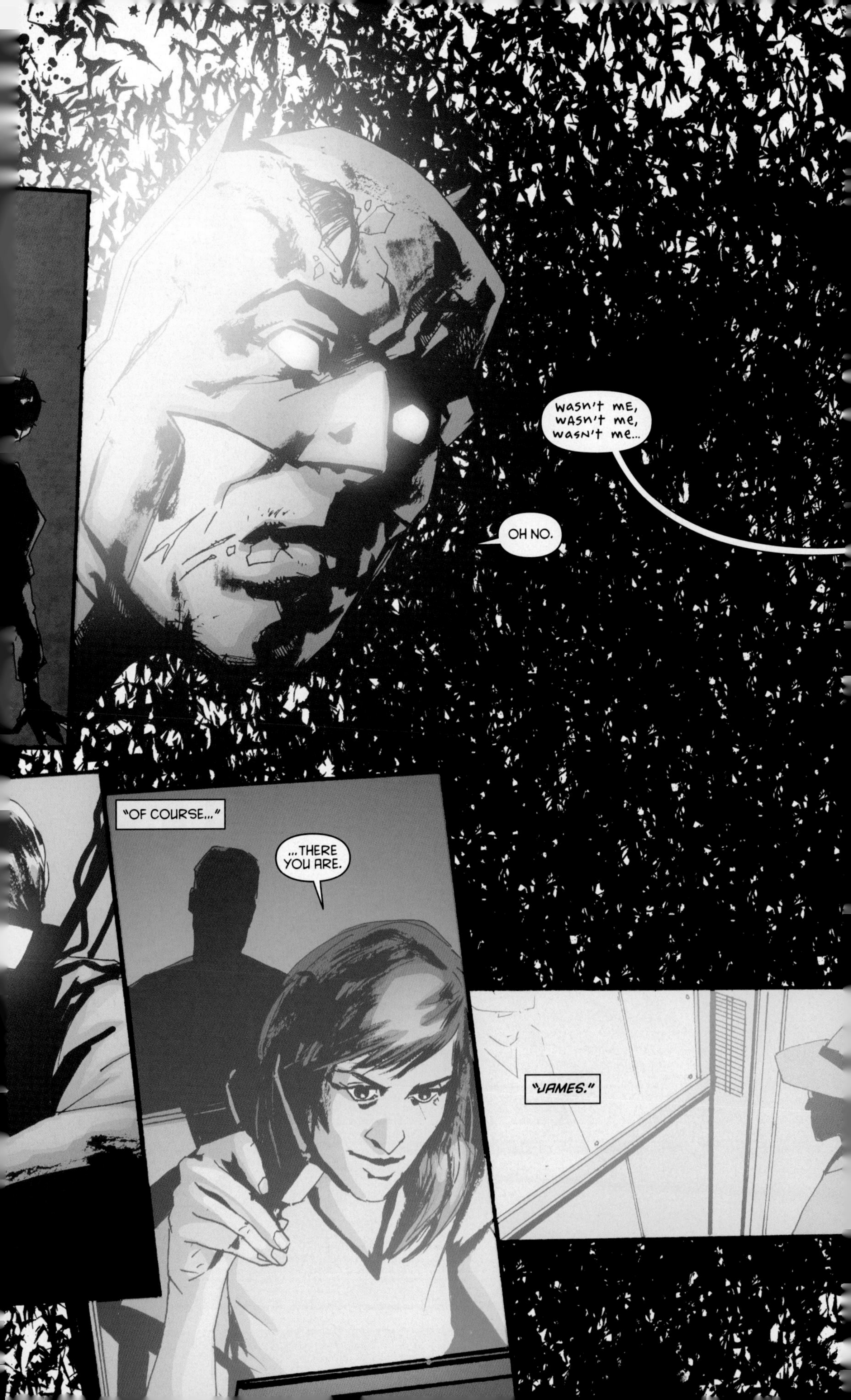
wasn't me,
wasn't me,
wasn't me...
OH NO.
"OF COURSE..."
...THERE YOU ARE.
"JAMES."

MY DARK ARCHITECT
HI THERE, SIS. AREN'T YOU HAPPY TO SEE ME?
Scott Snyde WRITE
Jock ARIST & COVER
DAVE BARO COLORS
JARED K. FLETCHER LETTERS
AAAAGH!

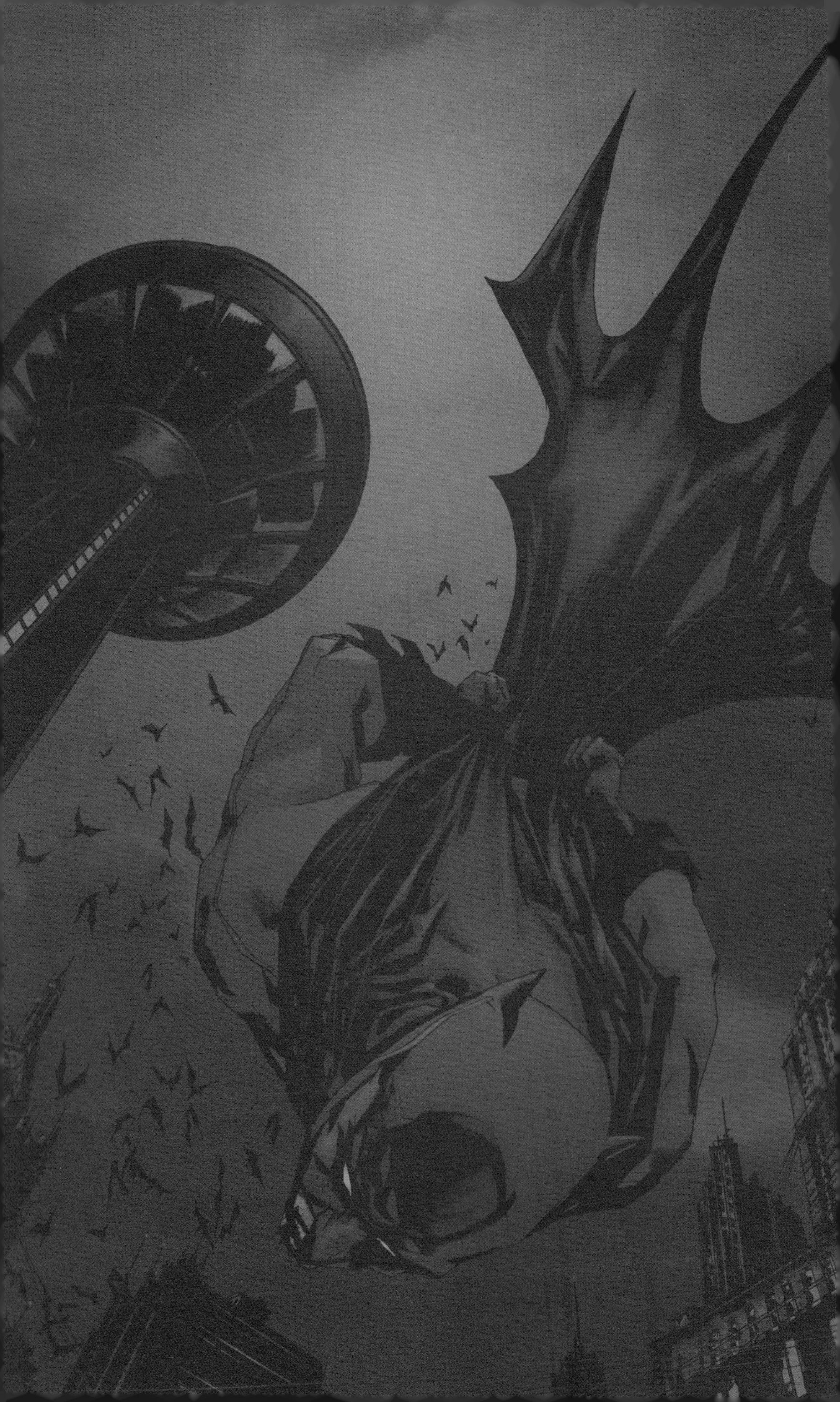

When I was a boy, my parents kept a big map of the country tacked to the wall of our dressing room.
AVIARY
BOARDING HOUSE
BOX DINER
CLINIC
The map had pins stuck in all the places our troupe was going to stop that season.
Different towns and cities were marked with different color pins.
Blue pins meant small towns...which meant small shows, less dangerous tricks.
Red pins meant big cities. So, big shows and more dangerous tricks.
All the stops were marked red or blue.
Except for one--Gotham City, which was marked by a black pin.
According to my father, the black pin meant no holds barred. Pull out all the stops. Bring down the house.
It meant put on the biggest, riskiest show of the season. No catch wires. No safety nets. Everyone pushing themselves to the limit.
WE'LL GET HIM, COMMISSIONER.

WE HAVE TO.
THEY FOUND *THIS* OUTSIDE THE KORD NEEDLE.

JUST SITTING THERE, ON THE SIDEWALK, WHERE THE TRASH COLLECTION COMES.
THE DEFENSES WERE ALL EXPENDED-- THE GAS, THE STUN CHARGE. SHE TRIED TO FIGHT HIM OFF.
THE DISCOLORATION--
IT'S *BLOOD.*
BARBARA'S BLOOD.
WE'RE THINKING THE SAME THING. IF SHE'S LOST THAT MUCH BLOOD ALREADY--
LIKE I SAID...
...WE'LL FIND HIM, COMMISSIONER.
SHE *ALWAYS KNEW,* BATMAN. THAT'S THE WORST PART. SHE SAW HIM FOR WHO HE WAS FROM THE START.
I NEVER LISTENED TO HER, BUT SHE SAW...

"...SHE SAW WHAT WAS COMING."
HELLO, SIS.
YOU LIKE IT? I FIGURED WE'D GO OLD-FASHIONED TONIGHT. TAKE A ROLL DOWN *MEMORY LANE.*

THEY'RE GOING TO FIND YOU, YOU KNOW. AND WHEN THEY DO, YOU'LL NEVER SEE THE LIGHT OF DAY AGAIN!
YOU MIGHT BE RIGHT...I HAVE TROUBLE BEING AFRAID OF THINGS LIKE THAT, THOUGH.
HEY. WANT TO HEAR SOMETHING FUNNY? I THINK THE CLOSEST I'VE EVER BEEN TO BEING SCARED, EVER REALLY, WAS THE FIRST TIME YOU AND I MET.
CAN YOU BELIEVE THAT? IT WAS RIGHT AFTER DAD AND SARAH TOOK YOU IN. THEY INTRODUCED US, AND I REMEMBER, EVEN AS WE WERE SHAKING HANDS, YOU GAVE ME THIS... THIS LOOK.
LIKE YOU SAW ME. REALLY SAW ME, THE ME THAT WAS WAITING TO COME OUT. THE BAD ME, THE ONE HERE TODAY, I GUESS. HEH
I'LL TELL YOU A SECRET, TOO. SOMETHING I'VE NEVER TOLD ANYONE, BIG SISTER.
SCARED AS IT MADE ME, I WAS ALSO RELIEVED. RELIEVED THAT SOMEONE ELSE SAW IT, TOO. THAT IT WAS REAL.
I HATE TO DISAPPOINT YOU, JAMES, BUT IT DOESN'T TAKE ANYTHING EXTRAORDINARY TO SEE YOU'RE A PSYCHOPATH.
WHEN DID YOU KNOW, THOUGH? I MEAN REALLY KNOW?
WHEN YOU HURT THAT BUS DRIVER.
SHANISSE.
SHE'D PICKED ON YOU ONE TIME, WHEN YOU AND I WERE GOING TO THAT DAY CAMP.
SENECA OR WHATEVER IT WAS CALLED. SHE'D TOLD YOU TO HURRY UP ONE MORNING, CALLED YOU SOME NAME--
FOUR-EYES.
I FIGURED YOU'D REPORT HER FOR WHAT SHE DID. DO SOMETHING OVERLY CRUEL TO GET HER BACK--I KNEW YOU WERE CRUEL THEN. I JUST DIDN'T KNOW THE SCOPE.
BUT DAYS WENT BY. THEN WEEKS. AND YOU NEVER DID ANYTHING. I REMEMBER THINKING-- THAT ONE TIME-- MAYBE I HAD YOU WRONG. MAYBE YOU WEREN'T SO BAD.

AND THEN, NEARLY A YEAR LATER. A *YEAR.* SOMEONE CAME UP TO HER IN AN ALLEY AND SLASHED HER FACE. DISFIGURED HER.
AND HOW'D YOU KNOW IT WAS ME?
THAT THING YOU USED TO HURT HER.
WHAT? IT WAS JUST A MATCHBOX.
A MATCHBOX YOU'D TAPED TWO ***RAZOR BLADES*** TO, ONE BLADE ON EITHER SIDE OF THE BOX, SO THAT THE THING WOULD MAKE TWO CUTS IN THE FLESH, RIGHT NEXT TO EACH OTHER.
CUTS TOO CLOSE TOGETHER TO STITCH.
BECAUSE IF YOU STITCH ONE GASH, IT PULLS THE OTHER ONE OPEN. IT'S A CRUEL TRICK.
POINT IS, YOU WEREN'T OUT FOR REVENGE, OR TO TEACH HER LESSON. YOU WERE OUT TO ***HURT HER*** FOR THE SAKE OF HURTING HER.
BECAUSE YOU ***ENJOYED*** YOU ALWAYS HA THAT'S YOU, JAM YOU ***WANT*** PEO TO PICK ON YOU.
YOU WANT THEM TO GIVE YOU AN EXCUSE TO DO WHAT YOU'RE DYING TO DO ALREADY...
...TORTURE THEM.
YOU'RE GOOD, SIS. REAL GOOD. HEY, TAKE A LOOK.
GO ON.

THEY'RE STUCK RIGHT IN YOUR FEMORAL ARTERIES. CAREFUL. IF YOU PULL EITHER ONE OUT, YOU'LL BLEED TO DEATH IN A MATTER OF *MINUTES.*
RIGHT
, THOUGH,
RE WEDGED
HERE NICE
D TIGHT.
SEE?
HEY, THAT REMINDS ME. YOU REMEMBER THAT TIME, BACK WHEN I WAS A TEENAGER, AND DAD THREW ME IN *ARKHAM* FOR A COUPLE NIGHTS, TO TEACH ME A LESSON?
DID YOU KNOW MY CELL WAS A COUPLE DOWN FROM *THE JOKER?*
THAT WAS DAD'S ROCK-BOTTOM, I THINK. HAVING TO PUT HIS SON NEXT TO THE JOKER, TRYING TO *SCARE* HIM STRAIGHT. CAN YOU IMAGINE?
THE THING IS, ME AND JOKER, WE ACTUALLY GOT ALONG WELL ENOUGH. HE'S GOT SOME GOOD ONE-LINERS, I'LL TELL YOU. *HEH* AND HE'S A *LISTENER,* TOO.
I TOLD HIM *ALL ABOUT* YOU, SIS. ABOUT DAD. I TOLD HIM THAT, IN MY OPINION, THE PROBLEM WITH YOU WAS THAT YOU WERE ALWAYS IN A RUSH TO *GROW UP.*
ALWAYS RACING AROUND, TO PROVE YOURSELF-- BE A HERO.
I MIGHT HAVE EVEN MENTIONED THAT, FOR MY MONEY-- AND OF COURSE, THIS WAS JUST MY OPINION--IT'D DO YOU GOOD TO *SLOW DOWN* A BIT.
TO TAKE A REST IN A NICE, COZY *CHAIR* FOR A BIT.

OF COURSE, I DIDN'T REALIZE HE'D ACTUALLY COME TO YOUR HOUSE AND... I MEAN, IT'S SOMETHING I'VE WANTED TO APOLOGIZE FOR, YEARS NOW.
YOU'RE LYING...
...YOU DIDN'T.
YOU'RE RIGHT, I'M JUST KIDDING! THE LOOK ON YOUR FACE, THOUGH...
AND HERE I THOUGHT YOU WERE DIFFERENT.
SORRY?
I SAID, I THOUGHT YOU WERE DIFFERENT... FROM ALL THE OTHER BIG BAD GOTHAM VILLAINS. AND BECAUSE YOU'VE BEEN SO FORTHCOMING, I'LL TELL YOU A SECRET.
THAT'S WHAT ALWAYS SCARED ME ABOUT YOU. BECAUSE I KNEW WHEN YOU CAME FOR ME THERE WOULDN'T BE ANY GRANDSTANDING. THERE WOULDN'T BE ANY SPEECHES OR CRAZY TRAPS WITH VATS OF ACID.
YOU'D JUST APPEAR IN MY BEDROOM ONE NIGHT AND YOUR HANDS WOULD BE AT MY THROAT. BUT I WAS WRONG ABOUT YOU, JAMES.
MAYBE YOU'RE NOT SO SCARY AFTER ALL. BECAUSE HERE YOU ARE, KEEPING ME ALIVE, GLOATING LIKE EVERY OTHER--

SCHLUK
NO, SIS. YOU WERE RIGHT.
YOU'VE ALWAYS BEEN RIGHT.
THAT'S WHAT I LOVE ABOUT YOU.
BUT SEE, I DID ALL THIS BECAUSE THIS TIME, IT ISN'T ABOUT YOU...
FRAN CAVIL LA '11

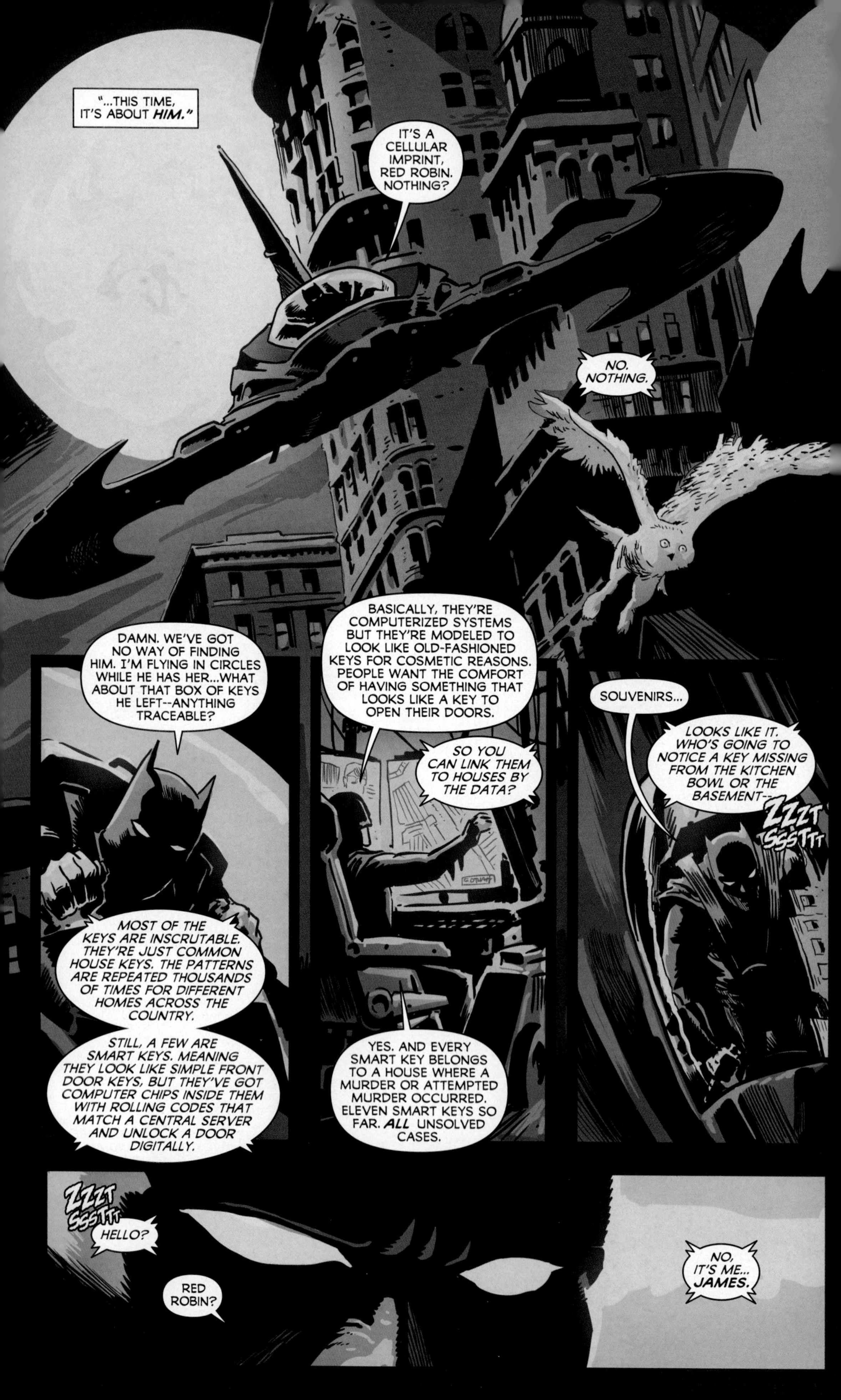
"...THIS TIME, IT'S ABOUT *HIM.*"
IT'S A CELLULAR IMPRINT, RED ROBIN. NOTHING?
NO. NOTHING.
DAMN. WE'VE GOT NO WAY OF FINDING HIM. I'M FLYING IN CIRCLES WHILE HE HAS HER...WHAT ABOUT THAT BOX OF KEYS HE LEFT--ANYTHING TRACEABLE?
MOST OF THE KEYS ARE INSCRUTABLE. THEY'RE JUST COMMON HOUSE KEYS. THE PATTERNS ARE REPEATED THOUSANDS OF TIMES FOR DIFFERENT HOMES ACROSS THE COUNTRY.
STILL, A FEW ARE SMART KEYS. MEANING THEY LOOK LIKE SIMPLE FRONT DOOR KEYS, BUT THEY'VE GOT COMPUTER CHIPS INSIDE THEM WITH ROLLING CODES THAT MATCH A CENTRAL SERVER AND UNLOCK A DOOR DIGITALLY.
BASICALLY, THEY'RE COMPUTERIZED SYSTEMS BUT THEY'RE MODELED TO LOOK LIKE OLD-FASHIONED KEYS FOR COSMETIC REASONS. PEOPLE WANT THE COMFORT OF HAVING SOMETHING THAT LOOKS LIKE A KEY TO OPEN THEIR DOORS.
SO YOU CAN LINK THEM TO HOUSES BY THE DATA?
YES. AND EVERY SMART KEY BELONGS TO A HOUSE WHERE A MURDER OR ATTEMPTED MURDER OCCURRED. ELEVEN SMART KEYS SO FAR. ***ALL*** UNSOLVED CASES.
SOUVENIRS...
LOOKS LIKE IT. WHO'S GOING TO NOTICE A KEY MISSING FROM THE KITCHEN BOWL OR THE BASEMENT--
ZZZT SSSTTT
ZZZT SSSTTT
HELLO?
RED ROBIN?
*NO, IT'S ME... **JAMES.***

GORDON.
ARE YOU THERE, DICK? IT'S HARD TO TELL WHEN YOU USE THAT STRANGE VOICE. WOULD YOU MIND USING YOUR NATURAL ONE?
DICK? ARE YOU STILL THERE?
WHERE ARE YOU, JAMES?
YOU KNOW I CAN'T TELL YOU THAT. LUCKILY, THIS SYMMETRICAL ENCRYPTION YOU US WITH MY SISTER'S CONSOLE WILL SCRAMBLE THE SIGNAL.
SO NO ONE, EVEN YOU, CAN TRACE IT.
WHAT HAVE YOU DONE TO YOUR SISTER?
YOU SOUNDED SO SURPRISED WHEN I SAID YOUR NAME.
THE THING IS, WHEN SOMEONE'S KNOWN YOU WAYNES AS LONG AS WE GORDONS HAVE, IT'S NOT HARD TO PUT IT TOGETHER. I HATE TO BURST YOUR BUBBLE. RESISTING THE ANSWER IS AN ACT OF WILL, HONESTLY.
WHAT HAVE YOU DONE TO BARBARA?
YOU KNOW, DICK, THE NIGHT BEFORE MY MOTHER LEFT MY FATHER, THE NIGHT BEFORE SHE AND I LEFT GOTHAM FOR CHICAGO...
...I REMEMBER PEEKING INTO THEIR ROOM AND SEEING MY MOTHER AND MY FATHER SITTING ON THEIR BED, HER HEAD ON HIS SHOULDER.
AND I REMEMBER SHE SAID TO HIM, "I HATE THIS PLACE SO MUCH, JIM. IT'S A CITY OF NIGHTMARES." WHAT DO YOU THINK SHE MEANT BY THAT, DICK? A CITY OF NIGHTMARES?
I THINK SHE MEANT THAT RAISING KIDS IN GOTHAM IS TOUGH.
I'LL TELL YOU SOME-THING--EVEN THOUGH WE BARELY KNEW EACH OTHER AS KIDS, I'VE ACTUALLY THOUGHT OF YOU PRETTY OFTEN OVER THE YEARS.
I'M FLATTERED.
HONESTLY, I THINK IT'S BECAUSE OUT OF ALL BARBARA'S FRIENDS, YOU WERE THE ONE WHO ALWAYS SEEMED THE MOST DIFFERENT FROM ME.

"YOU ALWAYS WENT AROUND WITH YOUR HEART ON YOUR SLEEVE. YOU WERE GENUINELY NICE--THAT WAS THE THING. IT WASN'T AN ACT. YOU CARED ABOUT EVERYONE.
"AND ME...I WAS DIFFERENT.
"OF COURSE, EVENTUALLY, LIKE ANY KID, I STOPPED WORRYING AND JUST ACCEPTED WHO I WAS.
"I LEARNED TO 'GO WITH IT,' I GUESS.
"LAST YEAR, THOUGH, WHILE I WAS IN TEXAS, I COULD FEEL THE LAW COMING. I FELT BARBARA LOOKING FOR ME, TOO...
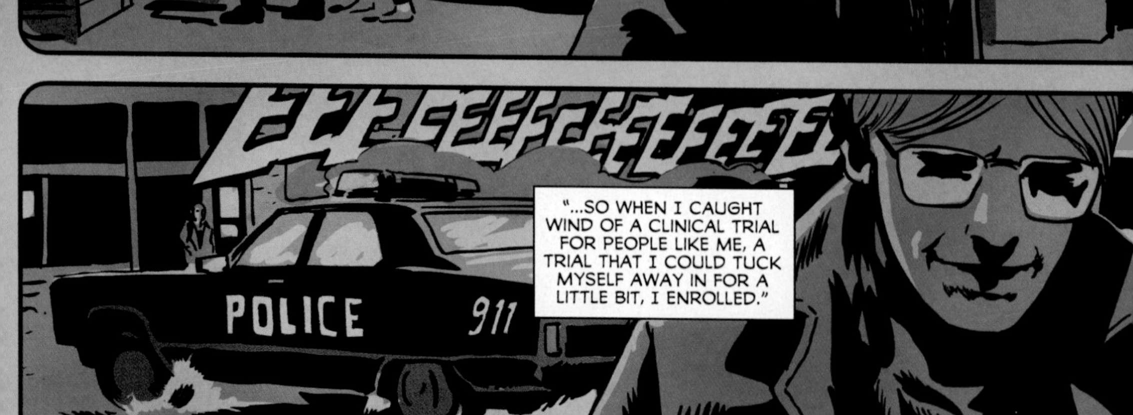
EEEEEEEEEEEEEEE
"...SO WHEN I CAUGHT WIND OF A CLINICAL TRIAL FOR PEOPLE LIKE ME, A TRIAL THAT I COULD TUCK MYSELF AWAY IN FOR A LITTLE BIT, I ENROLLED."
POLICE
911

"AND TO BE HONEST, I WAS INTERESTED TO SEE IF THE MEDICATION WOULD WORK.
"FUNNY THING, THE MEDICATION, THE DIAXAMENE, DID WORK.
"I ACTUALLY FELT THINGS, FOR PEOPLE. NOT THE WAY YOU DO, BUT A LITTLE BIT--A PINCH OF EMPATHY, I GUESS.
"AND IT MADE ME REALIZE SOMETHING. SOMETHING BIG. WHAT I REALIZED WAS...
"...EMPATHY, DICK--EMPATHY IS THE GREATEST HUMAN WEAKNESS. IT'S A HANDICAP. A VESTIGIAL LIMB.
"I SUDDENLY SAW IT SO CLEARLY, THERE IN THAT REC ROOM. ALL THOSE YEARS, I'D THOUGHT SOMETHING WAS WRONG WITH ME.
THAT I WAS DAMAGED... BUT NOW I SAW THAT IT WAS EVERYONE ELSE THAT WAS WRONG IN THE HEAD...
"...EVERYONE ELSE WHO WAS DYSFUNCTIONAL. BUT MEN LIKE THE ONES IN THE STUDY WITH ME, MEN FREE OF COMPASSION--WE WERE THE STRONG ONES. THE MORE HIGHLY EVOLVED.
"I KNEW IT. I KNEW I WAS RIGHT. BUT EVEN SO, I DIDN'T KNOW HOW MUCH LONGER I COULD GO ON THE WAY I HAD BEFORE WITHOUT GETTING CAUGHT...SO I WAS AT A CROSSROADS.
"YOU COULD EVEN SAY I WAS LOST, UNTIL..."
GOTHAM DAILY

"...GOTHAM CITY SENT ME A *SIGN.*
"A SIGN IN THE FORM OF A NEWS REPORT. A REPORT ON THE *RETURN OF BATMAN.*
GNN
BREAKING NEWS:
THE DARK KNIGHT

"THERE WAS THIS PICTURE OF HIM, OF *BATMAN,* AND HE WAS LEAPING DOWN ON CRIMINALS, BUT THE THING WAS, HE WAS...*SMILING.*

"AND ALL OF A SUDDEN I JUST KNEW. I KNEW THAT IT WAS YOU UNDER THE MASK.
"NOT BRUCE. *YOU.*

PATIENT NAME: GORDON, JAMES JR.
"AND IT ALL MADE SENSE AT THAT MOMENT. I KNEW WHAT I HAD TO DO.
"SO I PACKED MY THINGS. AND I CAME BACK TO GOTHAM."

"MY PLAN WAS SIMPLE ENOUGH. MEETING WITH DAD, CONVINCING HIM I'D CHANGED.
HAM
ARY
GC
"I'D HEARD ABOUT THE DEALER THE LAST TIME I WAS IN TOWN. I'D EVEN ATTENDED A COUPLE OF RALLIES.
I BEFRIENDED THE MAN, ETIENNE. I BOUGHT SOME OLD JOKER TOXIN FROM HIM, AND HEN I SET HIM UP.
"AND I'LL TELL YOU THIS, DICK. STANDING THERE, NEXT TO YOU, I COULD FEEL HOW RIGHT ALL OF THIS WAS. IT WAS THRILLING!
"I EVEN SAVED YOUR LIFE, YOU KNOW.
"WHEN YOU FELL FROM THAT ROOF. I PULLED YOUR BODY TO SAFETY, WHERE THEY WOULDN'T FIND IT.
"IN THE END, ALL I NEEDED WAS A DISTRACTION, SOMETHING TO GET YOU LOOKING THE OTHER AY, SO I'D HAVE TIME TO GET MY SISTER...
"...GETTING THE TOXIN TO JOKER WAS AS EASY AS AYING AN ARKHAM GUARD.
"AND THEN FRAMING HIM FOR THE ATTACK ON MY MOTHER...THAT WAS SIMPLE, TOO."

WHICH BRINGS US BACK TO THE HERE AND NOW...AND MY MOTHER'S COMMENT THAT NIGHT, ALL THOSE YEARS AGO, SITTING THERE ON THE BED WITH MY FATHER.
HER ASSERTION THAT GOTHAM IS A *CITY OF NIGHTMARES.*
BECAUSE SHE WAS *RIGHT.* GOTHAM IS A CITY OF NIGHTMARES. BUT NOT THE WAY YOU THINK IT IS, DICK. NOT IN SOME SIMPLE, SCARY, BOGEYMAN WAY.
NO, IT'S A CITY OF NIGHTMARES IN THE TRUEST SENSE. BECAUSE WHAT'S A NIGHTMARE IF IT ISN'T A *WARNING?*
A DREAM SO SCARY IT MAKES YOU THINK--MAKES YOU CHANGE YOUR WAYS? *A VISION OF YOURSELF AT YOUR WEAKEST.*
NOW BATMAN-- THE *REAL* ONE--FROM WHAT LITTLE I KNOW OF HIM HE SEEMS DIFFERENT. MY GUES IS HE SHAPES GOTHAM OUT O AN OBSESSION. OUT OF SOM PATHOLOGICAL NEED.
BUT YOU NEW CROP--YOU, AND YOUR FRIENDS, MY FATHER, MY SISTER... YOU DO IT OUT OF COMPASSION. OUT OF EMPATHY.
OUT OF WEAKNESS... AND OUT OF ALL O THEM, DICK, YOU'R WEAKEST. THE WEAKEST MAN IN GOTHAM.
YOU SEE, THIS PLACE IS SPECIAL, DICK. IT IS A CITY OF *NIGHT-MARES.* AND I'M YOURS. I'M THE *FACE YOU SEE IN THE GLASS.* A MAN WITH NO CONSCIENCE. NO EMPATHY.
GOTHAM MADE ME TO CHALLENGE YOU. YOU AND MY FATHER AND BARBARA AND ALL THE HEROES WHO DON'T SEE THE TRUTH. BECAUSE THE TRUTH IS THAT MEN LIKE ME, MEN LIKE THE ONES IN THAT STUDY, *WE'RE* THE FUTURE.
WE'RE THE NEXT STEP FOR HUMANITY. WE'RE NOT DAMAGED WE'RE SUPERIOR. I AM *GOTHAM'S SON,* AND CITY MADE ME SO I COU HELP USHER IN A NEW GENERATION OF CHILDREN, TRUE CHILDREN.
UNFORTUNATELY FOR YOU, JAMES, WE FOUND OUT ABOUT YOUR PLAN TO SPIKE THE BABY PUNCH.
ARE YOU SURE, DICK? I'VE PLANNED EVERYTHING THAT'S HAPPENED TO YOU SO FAR.
HOW DO YOU KNOW I DIDN'T ADD THE MEDICATION--BECAUSE THAT'S WHAT IT IS, MEDICATION, A CURE--HOW DO YOU KNOW I DIDN'T ADD IT TO THE INFANT FORMULA DAYS BEFORE YOU FOUND THAT ONE SAMPLE?
HOW DO YOU KNOW I HAVEN'T *ALREADY DONE* WHAT I SET OUT

YOU DON'T. I GUESS YOU'LL UST HAVE TO WAIT DECADE OR TWO, AND SEE WHAT GOTHAM LOOKS LIKE THEN!
BUT LIKE I SAID, I'M HERE TO CHALLENGE YOU. SO HERE'S YOUR CHALLENGE. IN A OMENT, I'M GOING TO FINISH KILLING MY SISTER.
YOU'LL FIND HER BODY SOON ENOUGH. AND BEFORE LEAVING TOWN I'LL KILL MY FATHER.
AND MY GUESS IS, WITHOUT THEM, YOU'LL GIVE UP. BATMAN WOULDN'T. HE'D SOLDIER ON. NO MATTER WHO DIED, EVEN YOU.
BUT YOU CAN'T, DICK. BECAUSE YOU CARE ABOUT PEOPLE TOO MUCH. ABOUT YOUR FRIENDS. BUT THEY'LL BE DEAD.
AND THEN...THEN YOU'LL HAVE YOUR GOTHAM MOMENT. YOU'LL HAVE TO LOOK INTO THE MIRROR AND DECIDE WHAT TO DO.
SEE WHERE IT GETS YOU, YOUR EMPATHY. YOUR COMPASSION. TRY TO SEE THE BEST IN PEOPLE THEN.
NOW IF YOU'LL EXCUSE ME, I HAVE SOMEONE TO KILL...?

THAT'S THE *SPIRIT,* SIS! HIDE AND SEEK!
I LOVE THIS GAME. I PLAY IT ALL THE TIME.
AND I HAVE TO WARN YOU... I'M PRETTY GOOD AT IT.
SO I HOPE YOU PICKED SOMEPLACE HARD TO FIND.
BECAUSE HERE I COME...
...NOW, WHERE COULD YOU BE HIDING, SIS?

I'M DONE HIDING FROM YOU!
STUCK
WHUMP

OH, YOU SHOULDN'T HAVE DONE THAT, SIS.
YOU COULD'VE JUST TOLD ME YOU WANTED TO PLAY *TAG* INSTEAD...
...I LIKE THIS GAME, TOO. HERE I COME TO GET YOU, SIS!
HERE I COME!
I'M GETTING *CLOSER!*
AND CLOSER!
AND I'VE GOT YOU!
HEY, JUNIOR...

...CAN I PLAY, TOO?

WHAM
DICK--
BUT HOW DID YOU... HOW...
SHH
I'M GOING TO CAUTERIZE THE WOUNDS.
YOUR BROTHER AND I, WHEN WE MET FOR LUNCH, I PUT A TRACER ON HIM.
"I INJECTED A SUBDERMAL TRACER INTO HIS PALM. WORKS ON A CELLULAR PLATFORM.
"IT TOOK A BIT, BUT THE SIGNAL FINALLY KICKED IN MOMENTS AGO."
JAMES WAS RIGHT. I AM A SOFTY. AND I DO TRY TO SEE THE BEST IN PEOPLE...
...BUT THAT DOESN'T MEAN I'M STUPID.

ALL RIGHT, HERE WE GO.
COME ON!
BABS, STAY WITH ME! BABS!
DICK... DON'T.
DICK... DON'T LET HIM... DON'T LET HIM GET AWAY.
DON'T WORRY...

"...HE'S ABOUT TO HAVE A GOTHAM MOMENT OF HIS OWN."

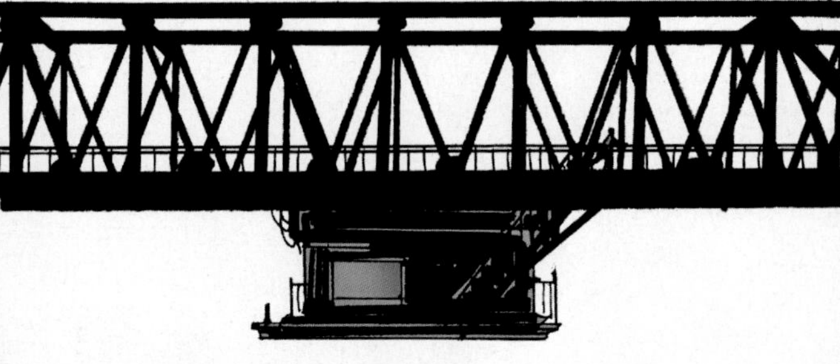

NOT THIS TIME, JAMES.
DAD, WAIT!
NO.
AAARGH!
BLAM
DAD... DAD...

I TOLD YOU.
NOT THIS TIME, JAMES.
I'M NOT LETTING YOU GO!

"NEVER AGAIN."
COME ON, YOU LITTLE PIECE OF... DAMIAN.
I HAVE TO SAY, I'LL BE SORRY TO SEE THIS PLACE GO.

COMMISSIONER.
ME, TOO. BUT WITH NO TAKERS FROM THE DEPARTMENT AFTER THIS LONG...I SUPPOSE THE IDEA WAS MORE *WISHFUL THINKING* THAN ANYTHING ELSE.
WELL, I'D BE REMISS IF I DIDN'T THANK YOU, DICK.
OF COURSE. IT WAS THE LEAST WE COULD DO, GIVEN--
NO.
I MEAN *THANK YOU.* ON ALL FRONTS.
YOU'RE WELCOME.
AND OUR LAST BIT OF BUSINESS?

RIGHT. WE RAN ANOTHER NALYSIS ON ALL THE ABY FORMULA TYPES VING THE PLANT THAT MES HAD ACCESS TO, BUT THE RESULTS WERE STILL INCONCLUSIVE.
IF HE DID TAINT THE FORMULA WITH THAT DRUG HE COOKED UP BY BASICALLY INVERTING THE DIAXAMENE REACTION, HE DID IT *LONG AGO,* LIKE HE SAID.
LONG AGO ENOUGH FOR ANY REAL TRACE OF THE STUFF TO BE GONE FROM THE VATS AS THEY STAND NOW.

SO WHETHER HE INFECTED HUNDREDS, MAYBE ***THOUSANDS*** OF INFANTS WITH A DRUG THAT COULD HELP THEM GROW UP TO BE SOCIOPATHS-- WHETHER OR NOT HE DID THAT, WE ***DON'T KNOW?***

MY HONEST OPINION IS THAT IT'S UNLIKELY. THERE WOULD'VE BEEN GREATER RESIDUAL MATERIAL.
BUT IT'S POSSIBLE.
IT IS.

-SIGH- THIS CITY...I'LL TELL YOU SOMETHING, DICK. SOMETIMES I WONDER WHAT KEEPS ME HERE. REALLY.
COMMISSIONER, THIS PAST YEAR, HERE IN GOTHAM, I'VE SEEN SOME OF THE MOST HORRIFIC THINGS IN MY LIFE.
THERE ARE TIMES IT ALMOST FEELS LIKE THE CITY KNOWS YOUR GREATEST FEARS, KNOWS--

YOUR ***NIGHTMARES.*** I KNOW.

AND HERE, TODAY, ALONE HERE IN THIS ROOM, I'LL TELL YOU THAT I THINK MAYBE THAT'S WHY I'VE AVOIDED PUTTING DOWN ROOTS HERE IN GOTHAM ALL THESE YEARS.
MAYBE DEEP DOWN, I KNEW HOW VICIOUS, HOW ***CRUEL*** THE CITY COULD BE.

THE THING IS, BEING HERE NOW, ON THE OTHER SIDE OF ALL THE TERRIBLE THINGS THAT HAPPENED THIS YEAR, I KNOW THAT THIS IS WHERE I NEED TO BE.
WHERE I WANT TO BE. BECAUSE I KNOW--LIKE YOU DO--THAT IF YOU MAKE IT THROUGH GOTHAM'S TRIALS, IF YOU CAN STAND UP TO THE MONSTERS IT THROWS AT YOU, YOU COME OUT REDEEMED. A STRONGER VERSION OF YOURSELF.
WELL, I FOR ONE HOPE YOU'LL STICK AROUND A WHILE THIS TIME, DICK.
I HAVE TO NOW. I'M STUCK WITH 4,000 FEET OF OFFICE SPACE I NEED TO CONVERT. I CAN'T IMAGINE SELLING IT'S GOING TO BE AN EASY FEAT.
the face in the glass
SCOTT SNYDER writer
JOCK & FRANCESCO FRANCAVILLA artists
DAVID BARON and FRANCESCO FRANCAVILLA colors
JARED K. FLETCHER letters
"SO WE'RE BOTH HERE FOR THE LONG HAUL."
"I GUESS SO."
"WELL THEN, ALL THAT'S LEFT TO DO IS HANG OUR HATS, BELLY UP TO THE BAR, AND BE READY FOR WHAT COMES NEXT."
the end

BATMAN: THE BLACK MIRROR SKETCHES AND DESIGNS

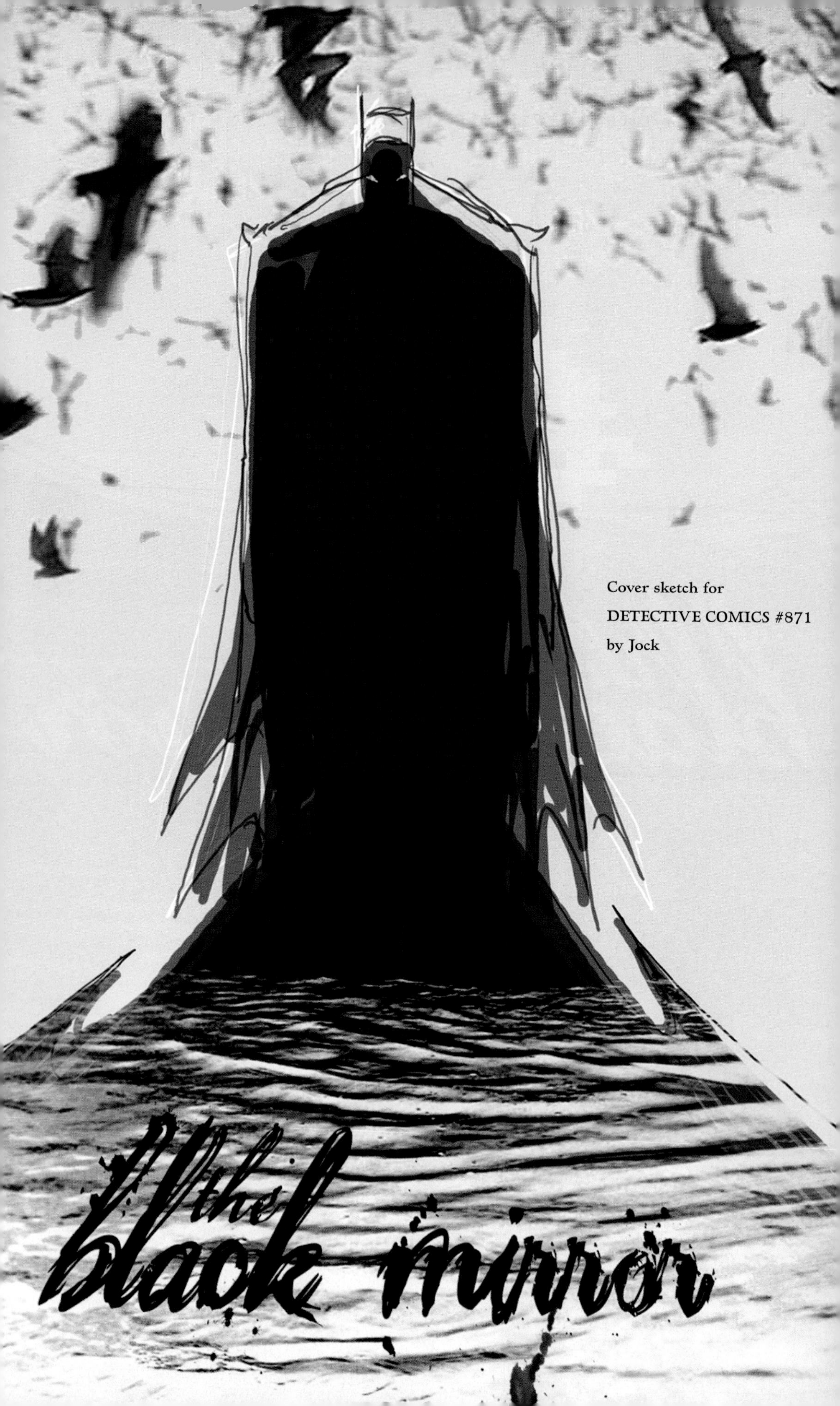

Cover sketch for
DETECTIVE COMICS #871
by Jock

Cover sketch for DETECTIVE COMICS #872 by Jock

Cover sketch for DETECTIVE COMICS #873 by Jock

Cover sketches for DETECTIVE COMICS #876 by Jock

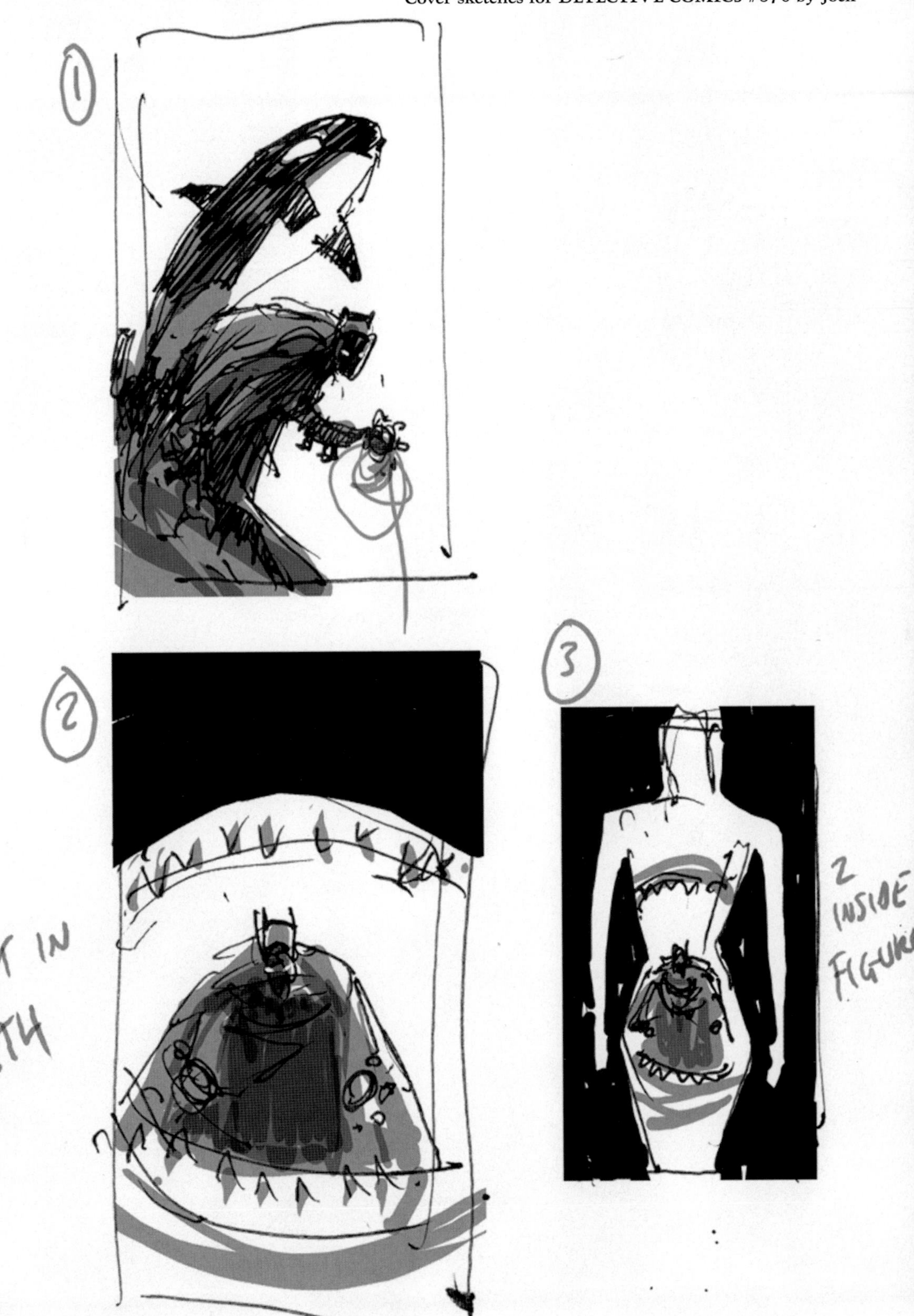

Cover sketches for

DETECTIVE COMICS #878 by Jock

Cover sketches for DETECTIVE COMICS #880 & 881 by Jock

Cover sketches for DETECTIVE COMICS #874 by Francesco Francavilla

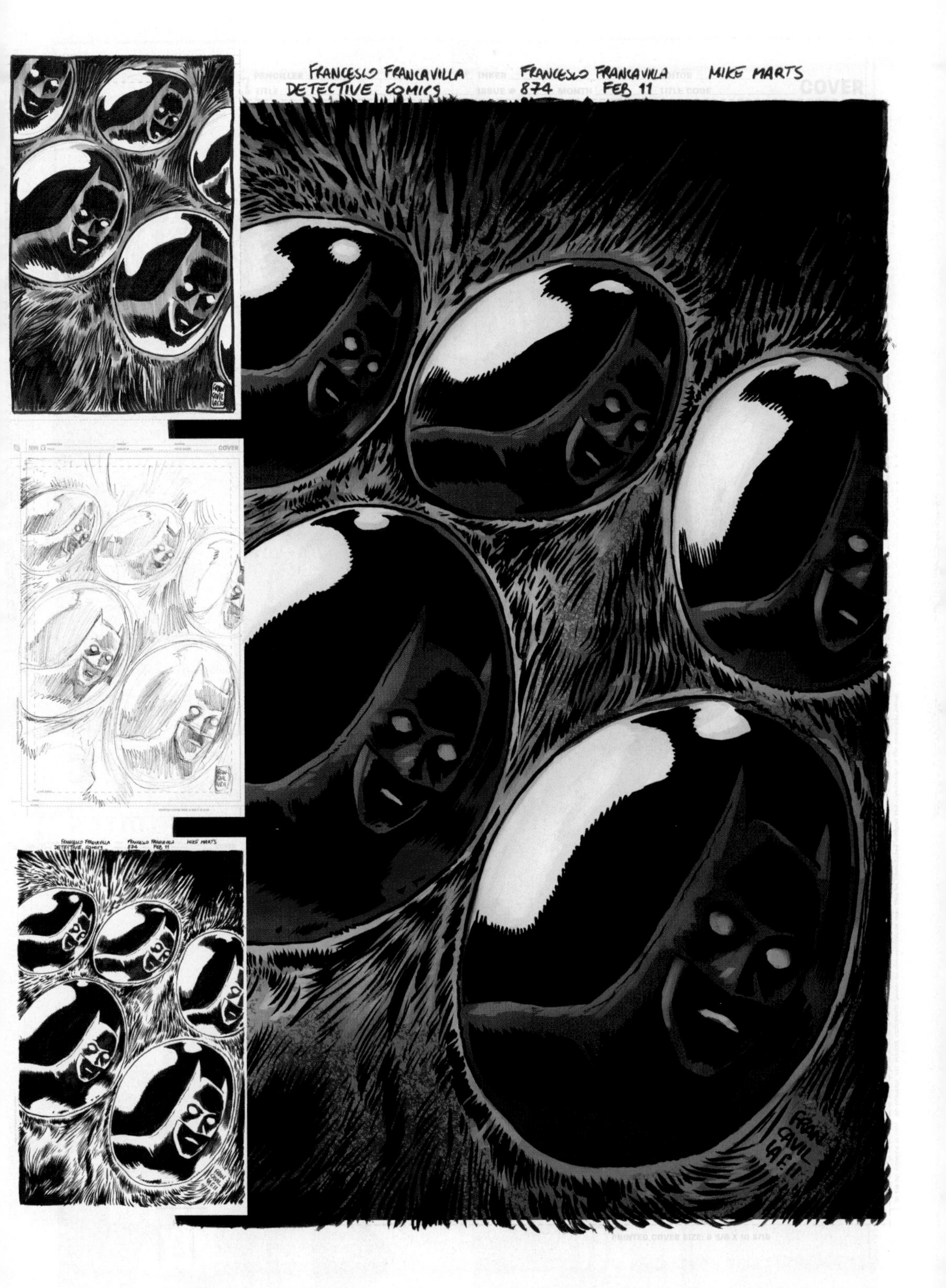

Unused cover and sketches for DETECTIVE COMICS #874 by Francesco Francavilla

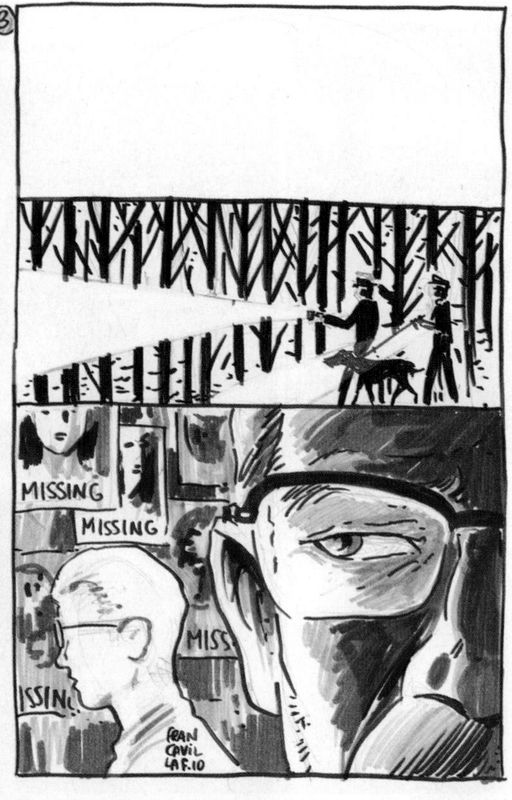

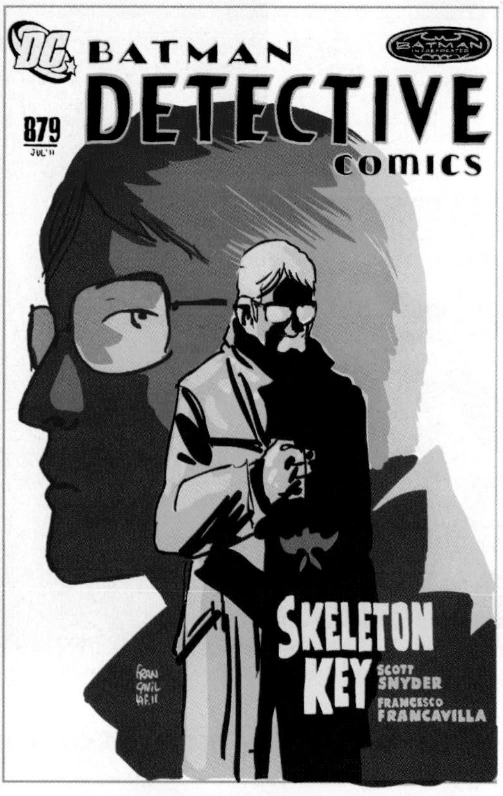

Cover sketches for DETECTIVE COMICS #874 & 879 by Francesco Francavilla

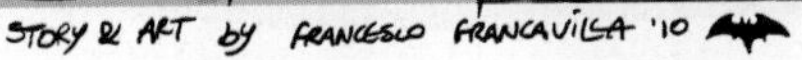

HE KNOWS ALREADY... WHEN **SCOTT** TOLD (BATMAN EDITOR) **MIKE MARTS** THAT I WOULD HAVE BEEN PERFECT FOR TELLING THE JAMES JR. STORY, MIKE REPLIED HE WASN'T REALLY FAMILIAR WITH MY WORK.

I REALIZED SOME CONVINCING WAS NEEDED, SO I DREW THE STRIP BELOW WITH JIM GORDON, HARVEY, AND BATMAN, AND SENT IT TO MIKE.

AND THAT SEALED IT: I WAS ON BOARD THIS DETECTIVE RUN. I AM SO GLAD I DID THAT STRIP, SO SO GLAD. :)

F.F.

LOBBY-CARD STYLE POSTER I DID FOR **SKELETON CASES** THAT WAS USED IN EARLY P.R. ON **DC COMICS'** OFFICIAL BLOG, **THE SOURCE**.

Detective Comics #871

JAMES JR. character design

SKELETON CASES

FIGURES 1 & ***2*** WERE THE INITIAL CHARACTER DESIGNS FOR ***JAMES JUNIOR***. WE ALL AGREED WE WANTED JR. TO BE MORE *"GENERIC,"* THE KIND OF PERSON YOU WOULD SEE WALKING DOWN THE STREET OR ON THE METRO AND WOULDN'T EVEN NOTICE HIM. SO I WENT BACK TO THE DRAWING BOARD AND CAME BACK WITH THE VERSION IN ***FIGURE 3***.

I ALSO DECIDED TO GIVE HIM GLASSES FOR 2 REASONS: ***A)*** THEY HELP TO MAKE JR. LOOK LESS DANGEROUS AND A LITTLE UNSETTLING AT THE SAME TIME. ***B)*** PLAYING ON SCOTT'S BLACK MIRROR THEME, I WANTED HIM TO HAVE GLASSES LIKE HIS DAD, SORT OF A DARK REFLECTION OF GOTHAM'S FINEST COP.

AND THUS JAMES JR. WAS (RE)BORN!

Page developments by Francesco Francavilla

Page developments by Francesco Francavilla

FRANCESCO FRANCAVILLA F.F.
DETECTIVE COMICS - IN THE BLOOD 879 17-18 JUL-11
INTERIORS

FRANCESCO FRANCAVILLA F.F.
DETECTIVE COMICS "THE FACE IN THE GLASS" 881 10-11 AUG '11

The following is the first-draft script by Scott Snyder for SKELETON CASES PART ONE that appeared as the backup feature in DETECTIVE COMICS #871. Seen in this collection on pages 82-89. This story is the introduction of James Jr.

DETECTIVE #871 - PAGE 23

23.1

CLOSE on a TRENCH COAT hanging in a closet, among a couple simple jackets and old police uniforms.

This trench coat is JIM GORDON'S iconic jacket. We're inside Gordon's apartment, and it's late at night, FF.

GORDON CAPTION: "These are the questions I get asked the most by people around Gotham..."

GORDON CAPTION: "And these are my answers."

23.2

CLOSE on a FRAMED DET OF 5 BADGES, showing Gordon's progression from an officer in Chicago to commissioner in Gotham:

BADGE 1: POLICE OFFICER: CHICAGO DEPT. OF POLICE.

BADGE 2: DETECTIVE: CHICAGO DEPT. OF POLICE.

BADGE 3: LIEUTENANT: GOTHAM CITY POLICE DEPT.

BADGE 4: CAPTAIN: GOTHAM CITY POLICE DEPT.

BADGE 5: COMMISSIONER: GOTHAM CITY POLICE DEPT.

The inscription at the bottom of the framed mementos: *"Happy Father's Day to an Unlawfully Great Dad, Love, Babs."*

GORDON CAPTION: "'You ever shot anyone?' And my answer is, 'Too many times.'"

GORDON CAPTION: "'You ever been shot?' And my answer is, 'Too many times.'"

GORDON CAPTION: "And the question I get the most... 'How do you leave it all behind when you go home?' My answer to this one is: 'You learn to block it out.'

23.3

CLOSE on a set of FRAMED ARTICLES from the Gazette, and others, showing Gordon triumphant at the end of notable cases. One article could be by Vicki Vale.

HEADLINE 1: Clown Prince's Plot to Poison Reservoir Foiled by Intrepid Police Lieutenant.

HEADLINE 2: Police Department's War on Organized Crime a Success: Maroni and Falcone Families in Shambles After Series of Bold Convictions.

GORDON CAPTION: "But that's not the truth."

GORDON CAPTION: "The real truth is that when you've been doing this as long as I have – you don't leave it behind. You can't."

SFX (TELEPHONE – OFF PANEL): RING.... RING....

23.4

CLOSE on 3 FRAMED PHOTOS OF THE GORDON FAMILY on a shelf. The photos move backwards through time, left to right.

PHOTO 1: Gordon and Barbara, recently. He's standing behind her chair. They're posing together, smiling on a sunny day.

PHOTO 2: Gordon (back when his hair was red), Sarah Essen and a young, teenaged Barbara, smiling for the camera at the zoo.

PHOTO 3: This photo is set back from the others, notably in the shadows. Almost as though Gordon isn't sure to keep it up on the shelf anymore. It shows an even earlier scene – Gordon as a young man, hair bright red, holding a BABY BOY in his arms – like a 1-year-old, just old enough to see that this is a boy. This is JAMES JR. (Gordon's son, from continuity, as in Year One). We will see more of him soon... Barbara stands beside the two, a cute little girl, about 4 years old.

[NOTE: The continuity is conventional canon: Gordon was married to Barbara Sr. early on in his career, from Chicago to Gotham. They had James Jr. in Gotham. Jim's niece, Babs, sometimes visited (hence the early picture). After the divorce, James Jr. went with Barbara, and Jim eventually married Sarah Essen. The two of them adopted Babs as their daughter when she was a young teen. Nothing new.]

GORDON CAPTION: "Because no matter how good you think you are at drawing a line between work and home, there will always be some cases that stay with you..."

GORDON CAPTION: "Cases that come howling back at you out of the darkness, like phone calls in the middle of the night."

SFX: RING... RING...

DETECTIVE #871 - PAGE 24

24.1

We're inside Gordon's bedroom now. JIM GORDON is sitting in bed, his back to us, holding the phone to his ear. Gordon is in his undershirt and boxers. This is a war-wagon of a man – still solid and strong, imposing, but also weathered, shoulders worn down by time.

SFX: RIN-

GORDON: Gordon.

24.2

Small - We're at the other end of the line with HARVEY BULLOCK. He's standing in the GOTHAM AVIARY. But this isn't important to show here, unless you do a touch or hint of feathers behind cage bars or something.

BULLOCK: It's Harvey. I'm at the Aviary.

24.3

Gordon, standing, turning on the lights.

BULLOCK (THROUGH PHONE): I got something you should see.

GORDON: I'm listening.

24.4

Small – on BULLOCK, as he cradles the phone a bit, almost like he's trying to keep the call secret.

BULLOCK: Jim, I think it's something *you should see.* For yourself?

24.5

Gordon standing before his closet, with the trench coat inside, reaching for the coat.

GORDON: (sigh) I'll be there in fifteen.

DETECTIVE #871 - PAGE 25

25.1

Large – Gordon being led by Bullock into the GOTHAM AVIARY, a zoo for the world's most exotic birds. Most of which are now returned to their cages. It's late at night, and a COUPLE OF WORKERS are sweeping up, maybe closing the doors to a cage or two, now that the birds are mostly back. These are things that can be happening in the background of the following panels, as Gordon and Bullock walk to the main office. Touches occurring in the background. Take whatever liberties you want, too, FF! If you think focusing on the birds or cages for a panel or two would be effective – keeping Gordon and Bullock in the background, the workers/birds in the foreground I'm fine with it. Or, if you'd rather focus on Gordon and Bullock walking, keep the birds and aviary activity in the back, fine. The feeling should be tribal and creepy, animalistic – Gotham is changing, becoming more hungry and vicious and adapting to challenge Dick Grayson and Jim Gordon both.

BULLOCK: So sometime around six in the evening, just after closing, the cages in the aviary sleeping quarters unlocked.

25.2
Bullock leading Gordon past the cages. Gordon is tired, could be rubbing his eye or something.

BULLOCK: Now Mayor Hady, he's all hot and bothered, see, because he has these dignitaries from some God-forsaken desert hole visiting Gotham this week and what's their first stop?

GORDON: The aviary. Harvey… It's late. I get the politics, but we got a felony "cruelty to animals" at best here.

25.3
Bullock, still leading Gordon past the cages.

BULLOCK: Just listen.

BULLOCK: The cages in this place are all automated. They're controlled by the aviary's main computer system.

DETECTIVE #871 - PAGE 26

26.1
Large - They enter a control room. There's an OFFICER manning the station. It's all surveillance – screens showing various parts of the aviary.

BULLOCK: Which means some time before closing, our guy snuck into the control room unnoticed, reprogrammed the cages, and set all the birds free-willy to flap around Gotham.

BULLOCK (TO THE OFFICER): A little privacy, pal?

OFFICER (DAN): Sure thing. Evening, Commissioner.

GORDON: Dan.

26.2
The guard leaving in the background as the two cops watch the footage in the fore.

BULLOCK: So Hady, he sends me and my guys down here to look over the surveillance footage.

BULLOCK: See if we spy anyone suspicious coming out of the aviary toward the end of the day. Choice assignment, right?

26.3
CLOSE on a SCREEN (grainy security monochromatic footage) showing a man walking out of aviary. If you want to show Harvey's hand in the panel, pointing, that's fine. The footage here should look like surveillance footage shot from a camera mounted above the exit gates of the main hall. So the angle should be high, looking down at people moving out of the hall, toward the exits. Among the people moving is a MAN, moving slowly. Taking his time. He is a plain-looking person, really. Slim, average height. Pants and a light jacket. Hair parted to the side (his hair is brownish red, though we can't see that here).

BULLOCK (OFF-PANEL): Anyway, I'm looking through the last hour of tape, barely paying attention, until I notice this guy exiting the main hall real late, right at closing.

26.4
Small - CLOSE on Gordon's face – he looks stunned, mouth open just slightly, eyes narrowed. Bullock is watching him.

BULLOCK (OFF-PANEL): You're seeing who I'm seeing, Jim?

26.5
Small - CLOSER on the MAN. He has paused. People are walking past him in a blur. But he's standing still. He is now beginning to look up at the camera.

BULLOCK (OFF-PANEL): Jim?

26.6
Small - EXTREMELY CLOSE on the man, who's now looking at the camera, smiling very, very slightly. This is JAMES JR., Jim Gordon's troubled son. He should look like a young version of Gordon, late 20s, but without the mustache. A nice-looking, trim, clean-cut man with glasses (maybe) and a slight, kind smile.

He should be wearing plain clothes. He dresses a little preppy, but casual. Khakis, a wind-breaker, a plain button-down beneath. Not cool. He's the kind of guy you wouldn't notice. He blends into the crowd. Get close to him, and there's something just a little creepy about his smile, something cold and vapid. Like he only smiles with his mouth, while his eyes keep the same calm, but alert stare all the time. In fact, I think it might be good to draw his eyes –which are a clear, light blue – with pupils that are always very contracted – tiny pinpoints of black (black pins, like the reference in the opening captions of the feature...). He looks like a nice young man, with something maybe just a tiny bit off about him, a little too intense...

[NOTE: Francesco – this is the star of your story. We're going to make him one of the scariest mothers in the DCU. The idea is that he is a true psychopath – devoid of empathy. He's been away for a long time, wandering, staying away. No one knows where he has been, but his last encounter with Jim was bad – years ago. Jim has always known something was "wrong" with him, but how wrong is a mystery to him. That's the idea: James Jr. is the worst thing Jim could have for a son – an unsolvable mystery. Jim cannot figure out what Babs (one of the very smartest in the Bat-family) knows instinctually – that James isn't just someone with an anti-social personality disorder. He's a killer. A true psychopath.
For Jim, the evidence is never there, and even the reason for James' nature is a mystery to him. Was it the fall from the bridge that damaged him? Was it the fact that Jim worked long hours, and wasn't around? Was he just born that way? Or was it... Gotham? James is the twisted, mirror reflection of Dick and Jim, in that Dick is all about empathy and compassion; James has neither. Jim is all about solving things; James is unsolvable...
Let's have some fun.]

BULLOCK (OFF-PANEL): Jim...

DETECTIVE #871 - PAGE 27
27.1
An establishing shot of Gordon's apartment. It's still night – raining now.

BULLOCK CAPTION: "You want me to put the word out, Jim? Just in case?"

GORDON CAPTION: "Thanks, Harvey, no..."

27.2
Gordon, having just opened the door to his place, is now turning on the light.

GORDON CAPTION: "That footage is rough as gravel. You'd be putting the word out on a ghost."

27.3
Small - CLOSE on his shocked face.

27.4
Because on the floor is a bright TRAIL OF BLOOD... leading toward the window, which is in the background. If the window is visible here, there should be a dark SILHOUETTE on the shade, that resembles the shape of a man – like a man is standing outside Gordon's apartment, on the fire escape.

27.5
Larger – Focus on the window, as Gordon approaches. There's more blood on the sill, dripping down the wall beneath, as though someone dragged a bleeding thing to the sill and took it out onto the fire escape. And again, visible on the WINDOW SHADE IS A SILHOUETTE – it appears someone is standing on the fire escape.

GORDON: Who's here?!

DETECTIVE #871 - PAGE 28
28.1
Gordon, coming toward us, approaching the window, GUN drawn.

GORDON: Show yourself!

GORDON: James?

28.2
Reverse: Gordon's POV as he approaches the window. His hand should be reaching for the shade...

GORDON: James?

28.3
A mirror image of Gordon's hand reaching, his POV... But this time it's reaching for the handle of a boy's bedroom door. This is 15 years ago, a flashback, but should be an identical image to the one above. Visible through the crack, a young boy, 7 years old, in his pajamas, his back to us, playing with something we can't see. But there is blood on the floor...

GORDON: James...

28.4
CLOSER on his hand reaching for the shade now.

GORDON: James, what have you done?

28.5
Same image, but this time his hand is reaching for the little boy's shoulder. We still can't see what's on the floor, but we can see more blood... as though the boy is playing with something dead.

GORDON CAPTION: "What have you done?"

28.6
Small - EXTREMELY CLOSE on Gordon's hand at the shade.

GORDON CAPTION: "What have you done?"

28.7
Small – same image as the boy's face begins to turn towards us... Just a hint of his face.

GORDON CAPTION: "What have you done?"

DETECTIVE #871 - PAGE 29
29.1
SPLASH –SCREECH! The shade is up – a big shot of a HARPY EAGLE SHRIEKING at us from the other side of Gordon's window. The giant ugly bird has a dead rat in its claws, bleeding onto Gordon's fire escape. In the foreground, Gordon recoils from the predatory bird.

DETECTIVE #871 - PAGE 30
30.1
We're outside, on the fire escape, the bird flying towards us as Gordon yells at it.

GORDON: Go on! Get the hell out of here!

30.2
We're inside with Gordon as he shuts his window.

30.3
We're outside again, looking through the window at Gordon with a hand on his forehead, massaging his brow as he tries to calm down.

30.4
We're on the street, looking up at Gordon's window. And in the fore, a figure with his back to us.

30.5
Reverse: we're looking down a bit from a slightly high angle, at JAMES JR. He's looking up at his father. His face shows nothing maniacal or evil. Just strangely cold.

CREDITS:
"Skeleton Cases: Part One of Three"
Francesco Francavilla - artist
Scott Snyder - writer